That's What Real Men Do

How Real Men Interact with Women

Mikal Haney

ParkerHouseBooks.com

© 2017 Mikal Haney
All rights reserved worldwide. No part of this book may be reproduced, scanned, or distributed in any printed or electronic form without permission from the author.

This book is designed to provide information and inspiration to our readers. It is sold with the understanding that the publisher and the author are not engaged in the rendering of psychological, legal, accounting or other professional advice. The content is the sole expression and opinion of the author and not necessarily of the publisher. No warranties or guaranties are expressed or implied by the publisher's choice to include any of the content in this book. Neither the publisher nor the author shall be liable for any physical, psychological, emotional, financial, or commercial damages, including but not limited to special, incidental, consequential or other damages. Our views and rights are the same: You are responsible for your own choices, actions and results.

Book design: Parkerhousebooks.com
Printed in the United States of America

This book is a dialogue depicting my belief that unfortunately as a society over these many years we have squandered the love, devotion, wisdom and leadership that is right before our eyes. Hiding in plain sight, these character traits, while not unique to women, are thoughtfully and meticulously refined by women. Largely male ego and selfishness have historically created in men a decided unwillingness to accept women's knowledge, skills, love and, above all, their unwavering dedication to any task or passion before them. This ongoing archaic view and equally archaic treatment of women, in my opinion, continues to adversely affect our society.

~ *Mikal Haney*

Dedication

To my wife, Denise, the most wonderful and delightful woman I have ever met in all my years of life and travel. Her involvement in my life gave me the inspiration and desire to write this book. To say she is the love of my life and a most cherished companion cannot begin to describe her virtues. Simple words can never suffice to chronicle her love, generosity and graciousness. Each day of her life she continues to give more than she receives.

To my daughter, Tresa, who regularly amazes me with her persistence, perseverance and positive attitude toward life. Quite possibly one day she will be known as a notable leader of change for our human existence. More positive female influences in often a chaotic world are a good thing. She is a most thankful reminder of why God put me on this earth.

To Robin Kinsey, for if she did not first plant the idea, I would never have started the thought process necessary to launch this project. Her words *"You need to write a book"* and her encouragement on more than one occasion served as a reminder to me that each one of us should tell our stories whenever the occasion arises.

To my late mother, Eula, who taught me how to treat women and reminded me regularly: *"Mind your manners."* I'll love you always, Mom.

To my late sister, Patsy, who worked tirelessly every day to help others and who brought much laughter to many as "Peaches the Clown."

These women who know love, compassion, devotion and communication deserve the very best life has to offer as they unselfishly give their very best each day.

To my late Dad, Ed, who always answered my questions, always helped me and always insisted I follow the right path in life. He truly was one of those "Real Dads."

Preface

As you peruse the pages of this book, if you decide you need not continue reading for whatever reason, please skip to the final chapter, Afterthoughts. At the very least, you may find something among those pages worthy of your interest, even though close-mindedness may be one of your dominant traits.

Be absolutely assured that in no way do I intend anything written here to be insolent or without kindness. All the words written here are expressed with utmost admiration and sincerity.

To all males, "If you don't believe or mean the words you speak, then, please, keep your thoughts to yourself and your mouth closed. If your words are merely intent as pacification then please save your money and buy another book. Most likely unbeknownst to you, your meaningless empty words already fall on deaf ears.

This book can be valuable in relationships and everyday encounters with women in the course of one's day. Any opportunity for a greater degree of communication to glean experiences and knowledge from women can never be a lost opportunity. Albeit this book has much to offer every man, if you have difficulty understanding what you read here, *just ask any woman*."

This compilation is intended to assist the male gender in everyday contact and relations with the female gender. Keep in mind every man has some type of interaction with multiple women whether he is married or single. By example, he encounters women at work, women while traveling to work, sisters, aunts, sisters-in-law and of course Mom. Women are everywhere in our everyday lives and we men should be treating them with the respect they deserve, the same way we expect to be treated. Save for the obvious fact of procreation for continuous population. If women disappeared from the face of this earth, a male-only world could not continue to function. To put it simply, men rely on women to get through the day more than they will admit and, in many cases, more than they even know.

Women may find this book a valuable medium to enlighten their male companions or acquaintances with its contents and the possible effect it could have on their future relationship. It could be used as an informal reminder to the men in their lives who may value a future relationship. Along the way, women will add subtle nuances to what lies in these pages as only they can, which could serve to enhance clarity for their relationships.

Little is known by the male gender about what lives inside the hearts and minds of our female friends and companions. **Let it be noted now, I do not have any magical or mythical insight to read the innermost thoughts of women.**

What I do have is a sincere desire and determination to assure those unique persons, the women in our everyday lives, that they are one reason love is eternal and they are deserving of much more than they receive.

I will continue to work to let women know I believe they should be revered for their timeless tireless devotion in everything they aspire to achieve. They continue to persevere in giving without taking and most often fail to receive even a minuscule reward or acknowledgement for their efforts.

The intent of this book is to express beliefs, practices, experiences, and a view of life many women never experience and, sadly, a view of life most women do experience. Having lived to this date for a good number of years leaves me with opportunity to reveal my personal growth, resolve and learning. Do I have all the answers? NO, but I certainly do not mind asking for my wife's views and opinions every day. If your view, belief or practice does not impart what is bestowed within these pages, then please understand I mean no offense to your person by what you read here. Do understand that, for me, these words and actions are my purpose and my intentions. *"Utilizing what you read here may give you cause to acquiesce."*

I do not believe every man fails to recognize women's knowledge, capabilities and compassion. There are men that treat women justly and fairly. I do know, in my world I see men every day treating women with disrespect in all aspects of life. I daresay a larger mass of men with any type of authoritative business position over women rarely ever treat them with the respect they deserve. When the relationship is a marriage or a growing romance and we had all the evidentiary data, we would be staggered by the number instances of thoughtless, careless, and sometimes brutal treatment of women.

Please, follow with me through these pages as we go about each day, each month and each event. I'll share my views for what I believe is the only rightful place for our most cherished of companions.

Where, you may ask, is the rightful place for our most cherished of companions?

*Beside us, of course,
Because?*
"One really means one"
*Also
Equal is just that,* **EQUAL!**

*(Hint, it's still equal when women are leading, too.
They know the definition of equal.)*

How do you treat a Woman???????

Let's begin with:

*As an <u>Equal</u>
With <u>Respect</u>
With <u>Admiration</u>
As a <u>Partner</u>*

And the greatest of all, **with Love**

Table of Contents

Chapter 1
    Morning 1

Chapter 2
    Lunch 5

Chapter 3
    Dinner 10

Chapter 4
    Early Evening 15

Chapter 5
    Late Evening 17

Chapter 6
    Sleep Time 18

Chapter 7
    Sunday 20

Chapter 8
    Monday 23

Chapter 9
    Tuesday 26

Chapter 10
    Wednesday 31

Chapter 11
- Thursday 34

Chapter 12
- Friday 37

Chapter 13
- Saturday 40

Chapter 14
- New Year's Eve 46

Chapter 15
- Valentine's Day 49

Chapter 16
- St. Patrick's Day 54

Chapter 17
- Easter 56

Chapter 18
- Memorial Day 58

Chapter 19
- June Getaway 62

Chapter 20
- July 4th 66

Chapter 21
- August Last Hoorah 71

Chapter 22
- Labor Day 75

Chapter 23
- October Fest 78

Chapter 24
- Thanksgiving 82

Chapter 25
- Christmas 92

Chapter 26
- Her Birthday! 98

Chapter 27
- Anniversary. No. Anniversaries! 102

Chapter 28
- Surprise! Surprise! 107

Chapter 29
- Mother's Day 111

Chapter 30
- Father's Day 114

Chapter 31
- The Workplace 119

Chapter 32
- Afterthoughts 130

About the Author 151

Chapter 1

Morning

(The day is dawning.)

If you are a "snoozer" the alarm clock should be set some amount of time ahead, thus allowing for a slower, less brutal emergence from the depths of dreamland.

If you are not the snoozing type, then simply set <u>your</u> alarm a few minutes ahead of the time the woman in your life normally awakens.

Why do you need this extra time? This time is used to *very gently* arouse the sleeping beauty lying next to you. With each snooze time slot, you have an opportunity to converse in one fashion or another. Each successive time slot allows for a more relaxing stress-free stir.

NEVER, ever leave the bed without first giving her a soft gentle hug and kiss or whatever is an acceptable demonstration of your affection. A "Good morning, beautiful" or an "I love you" work very nicely, too.

Now let's discuss the time between waking and leaving for work. Numerous events occur in homes across America. My point being, there are a myriad of tasks you can accomplish to assure your companion you have her at the top of your list all day, every day.

- Take out the garbage
- Feed the pets
- Make breakfast/coffee (Serve breakfast!)
- Clean up breakfast
- Make the bed
- You might even help her select her clothes for the day. She will be pleased you have an interest.
- Gather her work-related stuff (briefcase, purse, keys, papers, umbrella, etc.)
- Start her car (clean the windows of ice if necessary)
- Prepare the house to leave for the day (alarm, garage door, etc.)

If you have children, you may need to juggle some of these tasks. However, juggling them across to the other person is not an option. A sincere heartfelt discussion will serve to decide who performs what tasks. Along life's path it helps to take some of those tasks done by your companion on a given day and occasionally do them yourself even if she previously agreed to split the workload. A surprise many times is graciously appreciated. Amid the scurrying about, ask her if she needs you to do anything for her today. Ask her if she wants to go to lunch as this is a good time to get on her calendar early.

BEFORE you leave the house, tell her you like her hair, her chosen attire, her shoes and, most importantly, HER! Don't be afraid to say you are not particularly fond of a certain pair of shoes or specific clothes. Maybe they are just not your favorite color or style. Maybe they are *her* favorite and you should respect that and let her know she still looks nice. Other adjectives that come to mind for you to use during this conversation are: gorgeous, beautiful, sexy, seductive, happy, warm, loving, helpful—anything that lets her know you care about HER and how she looks.

Be certain to walk her to the car. Open the door for her and remember to close the door as well. Before you close that door, give her one more hug and kiss to start the day. Remember to say, "I love you."

Once more, if you have children, don't shrug off the above practices and attempt to use your children as an excuse. You need to adjust.

Most of these suggestions can be accomplished in any environment, provided you are willing to accept the challenge and you truly love your companion.

Mid-morning

Mid-morning is somewhere between 9:00 and11:00, adjusting the time for your specific circumstances.

Call her. When she picks up the phone, you might say, "Hello, Gorgeous," "Hello, Beautiful,'" or "Good

Morning, Beautiful." Ask her how her day is going so far. Be open to discuss (this means to listen to) any issues she may have with her day. She might want to bounce some things around and get your opinion, or she may not. Ask her about lunch, as the schedule may have changed. Ask her if she needs you to do anything for her this afternoon. Say, "I love you" before you hang up.

Chapter 2

Lunch

(Your third opportunity of the day!)

Yes, if you are paying attention, this is your third opportunity of the day. Pick her up for lunch. Don't meet her somewhere. She will appreciate your making the effort to keep her from having to lose her good parking space, get in a blistering hot car, get in a freezing cold car, driving in nasty traffic or drive in nasty traffic *and* bad weather.

If it is bad weather, you don't necessarily need to get out and open the door for her, *although it would be nice*. At the very least, lean over and open the door from the inside. Say, "Hello, how is your day going? You look beautiful!" (or gorgeous, sexy, ravishing, luscious—pick one, but don't let her get into the car without you say anything at all).

Whatever the response is, remember two words: sympathy and empathy. Share her feelings and understand her feelings. If she is having issues or problems with her work, don't try to fix them, simply LISTEN to her.

If she wants help, she will ask for help. You can ask questions. DON'T criticize. You will find out what she wants to talk about by asking questions. If your questions don't get the responses you might expect, you're probably leaning toward trying to fix something, or being too critical.

She may likely ask if your day is going well. DON'T whine! You are an adult and should be able to deal with your own issues. Burdening her with your petty issues will only add stress and, if her day is not going so well, you will be unnecessarily burdening her if all you are doing is complaining. If you have realistic concerns or issues with your day, feel free to discuss them with her. Phrase your words with selfless articulation. Value her views and experience. If you do not, then you need to read the rest of this book or stop here and give it to someone with a more receptive mind. *Which at this stage could be just about anyone!*

Do not drive like you're obsessed with speed and recklessness. You will create an unfathomable environment for a relaxing midday retreat. Ask her where she would like to dine or if she would she prefer to run some quick errands and then dine. Many times it is much more enjoyable to get necessary little things out of the way so you can have a relaxing lunch. Let her decide where to have lunch. If she passes the choice to you, give her more than one choice.

When you arrive at the restaurant, don't shut off the car and hop out. Wait briefly, give her an opportunity to fix her hair or put on makeup. If she gives you the opportunity, go around and open her door, at least make the effort.

You should be the one to greet the restaurant host and indicate the seating preference. As you are walking to the table, don't take off and leave her to follow. Stand aside and allow her to follow the host. Yep, you're right, when you get to the table pull out the chair and, yes, offer to slide the chair in as well.

Other things that come to mind are:

- Help her take off her coat, and fold or hang her coat.
- When it is time to order, ask what she would like. She may prefer you to order for her. It's ok to ask, and above all be respectful.
- Talk to her during the meal; don't gaze around the restaurant.
- Keep the discussion light; don't try to solve life's problems over lunch.
- Tell her she looks great, compliment her attire, hold her hand across the table, and don't hesitate to tell her she is beautiful.

When finishing the meal, pay the check. Get up and assist her to slide out her chair. Retrieve her coat and help her put it on. Again, don't just walk away; allow her the lead. Open the restaurant door, and open and shut the car door. (*If it is raining, you won't melt.*)

On your route back to work or home, continue driving in a safe and relaxing manner. Ask her if there is anything you can do for her this afternoon.

After arriving back to work, once more in case you have forgotten, wait briefly for her to check her hair and makeup. Before she exits the car, say, "I love you." Make every attempt to open the door if the situation is appropriate.

Here are a few more nice things:

- Holding her hand while driving is both affectionate and comforting to both of you. Yes, you will need both hands to drive at times, but this can be accomplished without sacrificing safety.

- A perfect time to show her you care is during that wait time at a stop light. A quick kiss or, since you are holding her hand, maybe a kiss on the hand would be nice. Watch traffic and pay attention. You can do more than one thing at a time. Hey, you have no problem yakking on the cell phone while driving, so get real here. Besides the car behind you is watching you, and your actions may become contagious. Your act of love and caring not only lets your companion know you have her always first on your mind, it may even cause someone else to react favorably toward that special companion in his life.

- Discuss the upcoming weekend. Maybe it's a holiday weekend—are you going anywhere?
- Discuss your last trip. Tell her you enjoyed the time with her and that you value those times together.

    Lunch is a golden opportunity to relieve the morning stress and head off any possibility of afternoon stress if you are both going back to work. Feeling more relaxed will indeed be less stressful.

    The lunch hour also affords opportunities for numerous other activities aside from going to a restaurant. You may take a walk in the park or go shopping. *Yes, I said go shopping.* We'll discuss the shopping reference later. Nonhabitual experiences are good avenues to foster communications and discover new mutual interests. Take the afternoon off and enjoy each other. Forget about clocks and everything else for a few hours. If you have her feelings, her person, her trust and her love utmost in your mind, if she knows you care about *HER*, you will enjoy the abundant and dedicated love you receive from her.

    A few words to live by: GENTLE, THOUGHTFUL, CARING, EMOTIONAL, LOVING, and last, but absolutely the most important, SINCERITY.

Chapter 3

Dinner

(What about mid-afternoon?)

Call her mid-afternoon, but don't make it five minutes before the end of the workday. And when she answers, remember to tell her you love her. Mid-afternoon can be much like mid-morning, yet there are subtle differences and important points to remember, like making plans for the evening. You *could* copy the mid-morning exercise, but that would be **boring**! Remember those *deaf ears* we discussed earlier? Empty words can never replace true heartfelt sincerity. After you have told her you love her, ask what she would like to do that evening. Maybe get some quick shopping in before dinner? *There's that shopping thing again; be patient!*

Are you going out or staying in for dinner?

Going Out

Going out is a perfect chance for you to surprise her. Instead of asking her what she would like to do for the evening, you could announce: "We're going out." Maybe she does not feel like going out. She will tell you; however, letting her know you thought about it tells her you love her. If your lifestyle tends to have you going out on a regular basis, then choose a special place, maybe someplace new. There may need to be a quick trip home to change attire to dressier or a more casual. Maybe dinner and *dancing*? Perhaps something you don't do every day?

For dinner out, remember the practices we learned at lunch. Open her door, drive safely and carefully, don't trudge through the restaurant leaving her to follow, take her jacket, slide out the chair and don't gaze around the room. Even a casual evening can and should be romantic. Remember to say, "I love you."

Discussions during your dinner out should still remain light and relaxing.

Staying In

Staying in for dinner can be a whole new experience. For example, prepare and serve dinner to her for a change. *Oh, so now your excuse is she gets home before you. Not so fast!* You can tell her not to bother with dinner, as you will take care of it when you get home. So, you don't know how to cook? *Just another excuse.* You have choices. Read a recipe book, view the food channel, or you could even ask her to help you. You might find out she would be happy to help you with the dinner preparation. Both of you in the kitchen preparing dinner can be endearing, not to mention fun and exciting.

Okay, it's finally time for dinner. Going out or staying in, you are well on the way to a relaxing fun-filled dining experience. If you are going out and you have decided to have a casual dinner, ask her if she would like to get some shopping in before or after dinner. *YES, shopping!* If you have decided on a more elegant evening, then shopping is probably not appropriate for this occasion.

An early dinner gives the added advantage for a relaxing stroll afterwards. It could be a great time to simply talk, look around, stroll through the mall or wherever you may find a serene setting to be alone and enjoy the companionship. Outdoor malls are great for this activity as you can enjoy the evening air at the same time.

So, let's get to it. Shopping, shopping, shopping. Yes, it is going to happen and if you will finally open your closed mind and realize the most important aspect of shopping is simple: *time spent shopping is time with her, for her time spent with you.* She will even do some shopping for you during these excursions. Most importantly, you get to see items she is browsing and talking about, all the while she is likely asking you about your likes and dislikes. If we can pry open that closed mind a little more, then we begin to see: *Hey, I need to remember this when it's gift time.* Now that you have a basic understanding of the *shopping thing*, we'll get to the *gift* part as we travel further down this road.

Staying home for dinner should not relieve you of proper etiquette. You should still exhibit courtesy, kindness, love and passion.

Unlike lunch out, dinner discussions in the home offer a connection where you can delve into all sorts of topics from A to Z. It is a good time to find out if there are lingering work-related frustrations from earlier in the day. Give her freedom to discuss her day and vent if necessary. Remember, you are not trying to fix anything; you are listening. If she wants you to fix something, she will ask for your assistance.

Open a discussion on plans for an upcoming trip or holiday or begin plans for a future trip. The more often you discuss upcoming events or future trips, the greater probability of success with fewer setbacks and misunderstandings with schedules.

You can *go shopping* regardless of whether dinner is in or out. Or after dinner, how about a quick drive out of the city to get a good view of the stars, maybe a short stroll in the park or if possibly on the beach?

You should start seeing a trend here—communication, listening, discussion and *listening*. We'll talk more about listening later, but if you truly do listen, you will be amazed at what you hear.

Dancing

Dancing is an inspiring never-ending expression of your timeless love for her. Dancing also provides an excellent method to cleanse away daily stress. Ask her, as she may surprise you. She may not want to go dancing, but she will notice you made the effort to ask. Remember, do not just head off toward the dance floor—slide out her chair and take her hand as you make your way to the dance floor. Look at her while dancing. Her eyes will tell you if she is enjoying her evening. Speaking about surprises, don't wait until you are on the way to dinner and spring the surprise about dancing. She may want to bring along another pair of shoes. Let her know before you leave the house. She will appreciate the gesture.

Chapter 4

Early Evening

(That time shortly after dinner.)

For our purpose, let's consider early evening to be between 5:00 and 8:00. Yes, I know a lot of workaholics believe 5:00 is dangerously close to the middle of the workday, and for some 8:00 is either quitting time or after the dinner hour. What is a *dinner hour* anyway? For sure, dinner is one of those times to be relaxed, take your time, slow down, and feel calm and peaceful.

Early evening is an important time of day. What transpires during this period sets the tone for the rest of the evening and beyond and, if you have been a real jerk, the *beyond* may be *way beyond*.

Upon arriving back home from your delightfully fun and romantic dinner and dancing, open her door and carry her extra shoes. After you have changed clothes, ask her if there is anything she needs done before settling in for the evening. Get those tasks completed and then prepare yourself for the next day. The better your preparations in the evening, the more relaxed you are in the morning.

During summer time, the early evening allows for enjoyable outside time around the house. Your time may be spent doing some yard work, planting flowers, moving those yard tools back where they belong or simply hanging out enjoying the evening.

And you can make this evening time available to anyone desiring time from either of you. Get any lingering work things wrapped up or reschedule them for the next day. Phone calls, errands, friends or family may dominate this time and that may be unavoidable. Make this time as enjoyable as possible and, remember, as evening slips away so does your alone time with each other.

Every evening, strive to find that time when it is only the two of you. Are you going to find time every single night? Of course not. What you are hoping for is that, at the end of the year, you can look back and remember all those wonderful evenings you had together. As you look back, you do not want to be saying to yourselves, *"We need to set aside more time for us."* Sadly, by then, precious time is forever LOST.

Chapter 5

Late Evening

(Finally, a time for relaxation—hers!)

Those pesky chores are done. Phones are turned off, doors are locked and the world exists only within the walls of your home. Now is the time to rub her feet, legs or shoulders, and to hold her and tell her you love her as you begin a relaxing evening together. This time should be reserved for just the two of you; conversation should be light. If you watch television, make sure you both agree on the selection. You can experiment for yourself, but you will find out that action-packed movies or sports do not lend themselves to a serene and peaceful environment. Try it. Get relaxed and settled and then pop in that new movie: *The Last Day of Death and Destruction*. Your mood changes and the tension mounts. Maybe choosing not to watch television and maybe turning in early is the mutually agreeable choice. Many times, an early night locked away from the rest of the world can be a relaxing and gratifying experience. Remember, slow, gentle, soft, caring, and with emotion. You have several hours; what's the rush?

Chapter 6

Sleep Time

(Depends on Chapters 1 through 5 and 7 through 30.)

Now you have completed Chapters 1 through 5, and we are about to wrap up one day, so it's time to get a clue.

If your male prowess, style, ego or maybe plain ignorance tells you bedtime is playtime for you, then your vim and zest may be leading you astray. I suggest you skip this chapter and come back here after you have completed the remainder of this book.

Everything within these pages is important to any relationship at some point in the relationship. We will discuss numerous aspects of how women should be treated, some thoughts to ponder, some to use or some for you to ignore if you choose. If you need help understanding what is the most important part of your life together, I know your most *cherished of companions* will be happy to help, because helping you is what she does every day.

What happens behind closed doors or when the lights go out belongs solely to you, her and your relationship. You cannot hide from the light in darkness. Motives of the heart will always be exposed. The manner in which you choose to treat her at this intimate moment is pinnacle in shaping the future of our civilization. Men teaching sons to respect women, the right way to treat women, can and will change the face of our existence.

If your "late evening" resulted in no television or a let's-turn-in-early sort of an evening, the intimate part will take care of itself. If your "late evening" did not conclude with an early retreat because of something you did or should have done, then try to find out why. Ask. If selfish actions took over, learn from your mistakes and make a vow to improve.

One important thing to remember regardless of which route your evening traveled, do not go to sleep without a hug, a kiss and saying, "I love you." *Remember, we are not promised one second into the future.* Regret is something you experience when it is too late.

Ok, you decided to read on, so maybe you expected more? There is more—more love, understanding, feeling, respect, believing, compassion and learning. It all begins when you finally realize she is the one that makes your world go around. You may still be in denial or you may not be ready to realize a good thing when you see it. Even with all the things she does for you, when you do little or nothing for her, *she will still be there for you.*

Chapter 7

Sunday

(Church? And let her sleep in a little, too.)

If you go to church, then please go. If you don't go to church, I understand it is a personal choice and not a choice anyone can make for you. Regardless of your choosing on Sunday morning, ensure she gets the opportunity to sleep in for a while. Ask her what time she needs to awaken to prepare for the day's activities. Before going to sleep the night before, be sure you asked her what she would like for breakfast. Give her plenty of time to rest and keep the remainder of the house quiet. You made all the necessary preparations last evening so now you can use this quiet time to indulge in a personal pastime. You could sleep in as well if you so desire. Why leave that sleeping beauty alone?

Clean up the breakfast mess before leaving home. It may surprise you to see she pitches in to help. Strange as it may seem, when you engage in such activities, you soon begin to see reciprocation.

If you are preparing for your day, remember to tell her how nice she looks after she dresses. This day should be the most relaxing, refreshing, stress-free day possible. Mind the driving etiquette. It's only

Sunday morning. Have you forgotten last week already?

After your morning activities, a lunch with friends or family can help to soothe the soul. Some Sunday afternoon shopping works well to top off the day, maybe a new dress for next Sunday, new shoes for those evening walks or simply window shopping. Go to the park, take in a movie. *Relax!*

Ah, relaxing at home. Get some planting in and fix some of those *"I need to fix that"* things. Clean out her car, maybe wash and vacuum her car. Round up everything for work early so you both can enjoy the evening.

Having a light dinner on Sunday gives you more time for family, friends and each other.

Sunday evening is the best day of the week to relax and enjoy life. Don't get involved in any deep philosophical discussions that would only create stress. Talk to one another and be mindful that communication is likely the most important thing to remember in any relationship, either at work or play. There is no such thing as "too much communication."

A phrase we sometimes hear is *"That person talks too much."* Usually this means the person making the statement is not listening, or the person talking likes to hear themselves talk and probably doesn't listen well either. Communication as defined in this context as an exchange or rapport between two persons. Never is it described as being one way. You can convey your situation or feelings to anyone about anything. If your words are not heard, then there is no communication. The flip side of you talking is (Yep, you guessed it!) *listening.* We will discuss more on listening later.

Sunday is a day of rest for all, and the more we practice this, the more time we have to get to know our loved one's needs and desires. And, remember, the tone we set on Sunday is what we begin with on Monday.

Chapter 8

Monday

(Time for those little before-work chores.)

Monday can be a tough day for a lot of people. You had a great weekend and now back to work. *What a drag! Or, an opportunity?* Cheer up! The weekend will be here soon, and you have all week to plan for its arrival. Time to do those chores we need to do each morning. If you prepared well last evening, then guess what, your life just got a little easier.

The ease and care with which you awaken your companion can make the difference between her arousing from a restful sleep or being roused. This applies not only to Monday. Never begin her day or your day with the potential for angst. After all, you are awakening a sleeping beauty, so be the *Prince.*

Make those telephone calls to her during the day with sincerity. Be especially empathic since it is Monday, and remember that you're listening, not fixing. Strive to make Monday a good day for both of you. After all, it will soon be the weekend, and fun awaits us on the weekend.

Monday evenings are important as you have before you a blank slate to set the tone for the entire week. Accomplishing all the chores early sets the stage for an unanticipated advance into the *quiet zone*. The quiet zone is that time when your whole world exists only within the four walls of your home. On Mondays especially, escaping quickly into this environment makes the remainder of the week more enjoyable and less formidable.

Be unpredictable. Here are some tips to help electrify a drab Monday.

You can send flowers occasionally or buy a card and place it in her purse or briefcase for a delightful discovery later in the day. Send her an e-card or break the mold and call her more than once during the morning or afternoon and say to her, "I'm preparing dinner tonight. What would you like?" or "I wanted to make sure I told you how nice you looked this morning." Maybe ask her opinion about a special situation you have at work (no whining) and listen to what she has to say. You will likely be surprised to hear the depth and range of her knowledge. Thoughtful words deliberately tell her you care about her, what she is, who she is, what she does and that she matters to you.

If you are not quite so up on a Monday morning, at least try not to bring everyone else down with your doom and gloom. After all, Monday is just another day, much like the other days of the week.

It may take a few minutes longer to get organized, but sometimes the weekend was a great weekend and you're simply recovering from the fanfare, so take it slow if necessary and remember that *niceness* is always good.

With careful consideration and appropriate commitment on your part, Monday evenings have a potential to be very romantic. Relaxation after possibly a busy stressful day can last all evening and into the night. Maybe a cozy shower, a relaxing glass of wine in the hot tub, or offering to rub some lotion on her feet and legs would be just what is needed. *Mind your manners*, and she will respond graciously to your thoughtfulness and sincerity.

Chapter 9

Tuesday

(Remember, you pick up the dry cleaning!)

After discovering on Monday what you may not have finished or failed to even start last week, now is the time to address those. Tuesday is the real first day of the week. Monday is really a catch-up day to organize the remainder of your week, which is typically why Mondays are jammed packed and oh so stressful. On Monday, you are trying to sort out where you are and making a strong mental effort to get on track. If you are organized, you made time Friday afternoon to prepare for Monday, and you need another good excuse why Mondays are so contemptuous, perhaps it's because they get in the way of good weekend.

Don't forget to pick up the cleaning. How many times has your significant other heard these words from you, along with asking her to do countless other chores you seem too busy to perform? Have you ever stopped to think about how much other people do for you? *Probably not.* This same scenario may be the way you act at work, too. *We'll get to that in due time.*

Unfortunately, many times these *orders* are communicated by a husband to a wife. *Communicated* does not necessarily mean *communication*. If you are so insistent that today, or any day for that matter, is "the day" the cleaning should be picked up, then stop and pick it up yourself. Chances are you will be driving right past the cleaners on the way to work and, unless you go to work at 5:00 in the morning, you can be assured the cleaners will be open. While we are on this subject, take time to do your own little tasks and errands. Stop relying on your "*Mother's replacement"* to do everything for you.

One day, you will be surprised to find out that she may offer to pick up that cleaning or do a few other tasks for you. When you do these tasks for yourself, not expecting her to do them for you, then you are telling her she is important to you and that she is not your personal valet. She is with you because she loves you. She believes you love her, so show it to her more often.

Monday is behind us and we are ready to get down to some serious work. During your *busy* day, check out the calendar. No, not for the time of *your next meeting*; you're checking to see if there a birthday coming up, an anniversary, another special day of the year, or perhaps Valentine's Day.

If you have access to an automated calendar, set up reminders like you do for your business meetings. Get in the habit of identifying the special days and adding a one- or two-day reminder previous to that day. If you don't have access to electronic devices or simply refuse to have technology infringe upon your life, then get a pocket calendar, set up those reminders, and check it every day. As for the reminder part, since you can't seem to get your own cleaning, annotate the appropriate day and for a few days preceding specific dates, place reminders on those days. Any way you prefer to attack the situation is acceptable. Just ensure part of your daily regimen includes checking your calendar. Look ahead for those days that may require substantial lead time for ordering, setting reservations, or giving that special someone necessary advance notice. Advance notice is required on certain occasions, which we will be discussing in future chapters.

Think about the week ahead and, more importantly, the weekend ahead. *Yes, I know you have work to accomplish.* You can type about 50 to 90 words per minute, depending on your manual dexterity. You speak around 350 words per minute. Your brain can process around 800 words per minute. There's plenty of time in there for other things. You seem to have time to discuss that golf game, some sports event, or how great you are at *whatever*. So, looking through the calendar a few weeks into the future won't take too much of your valuable time. Get with it! Think about the most **important** part of your life for a few minutes. It won't hurt and it will certainly help. (*Clue: t*he most important part is *your significant other.*)

Do some advance planning on your own, don't wait for someone (like your spouse) to do it for you or force her to inquire about some future thing you should already be planning.

There could be a long weekend coming up, or it might be a great time of year to take a long weekend. When was the last time you spent a weekend out of town? Look at your calendar. When is the next long weekend? How about just picking a date? That *calendar* you relentlessly check each day will have some extra room to write some notes. Pick a time, maybe this week, next week or next month.

Advance planning ensures you don't forget anything. And you see the best times and dates for some special weekend or surprise. *We'll talk more on the surprises later.*

You need to plan well in advance, and it's one of those things that will be immensely appreciated by your companion. Call her up. *You were going to be doing that anyway, right?*

Ask her if she wants something special for dinner tonight and go out somewhere in the evening. Announcing your intentions as "special" lets her know you are thinking of her and she is important to you— particularly if you tell her she is special to you and you wanted to do something to let her know how much she means to you. Simple as that, you surprised her. *There's more about surprises coming, so stay tuned.*

Tuesday is a good day for flowers. Why? So, you can say, "I love you," tell her what a fantastic time you had last weekend, or say, *"I'm thinking of you."*

Flowers speak volumes. Always include a card. Giving her flowers on Tuesday helps her feelings as the week goes on. I know we discussed maybe sending flowers on Monday, but remember that "special" is not designated for a certain day. You can send flowers on Tuesday, even if you sent flowers on Monday. *How special is that? Huh?* Think she will be surprised?!

Tuesdays are good for you to plan what you would like to get accomplished during the week, upcoming weekend and beyond, that is if you have been listening. There's that word again—*listening.* We'll get back to what listening really means. Ok, I hear you. *What about planning for me?* You can do that, but remember taking care of someone else and placing that person's needs before yours is the ultimate service to your fellow human being—man, woman or child.

Yes, you have much to say about your activities. However, if you were planning as we previously discussed, then Tuesday is a reminder day. You need to include all activities on your schedule, her schedule, and your "together" schedule. You don't want to fall into that miscommunication black hole. You know, the one where she talks, and you don't listen. Don't ever think for one brief second that, when you talk, she does not listen. She hears every single word. *You can take that to the bank!"*

Chapter 10

Wednesday

(A quiet evening out for dinner.)

Here we are in the middle of the week and hopefully it has been an enjoyable couple of days. Now it's time to firm up those plans for the weekend and any important future dates or surprises you have planned.

Of course, we don't need to inform anyone about any surprises lest we lose that important element. We will be discussing the appropriate time to give advance notice for surprises.

During your morning phone call, casually mention how nice it would be to go out for dinner tonight. You could wait until your afternoon call to spring the surprise, but telling her in the morning may serve to lighten a slow day and help to speed along her afternoon. Especially if you tell her the place you plan to take her is a surprise.

By telling her it's a surprise, you are likely filling her afternoon with intrigue while she wonders about this surprise clandestine rendezvous. As you are spicing up her morning with this news, you are telling her you continue to think about her even during your own busy day. Also, she gets to tell her coworkers and friends you are taking her out somewhere special.

Dinner out can be a great time for each of you for the opportunity to shed all that workday stuff, so you're not saddled with it after you begin to settle in for the evening. Remember to mind your manners while driving and at the restaurant. A casual conversation discussing your workday issues with a caring, listening soul mate can do wonders for your perspective of the day's events. You may even find your vision of how these events were handled is much different from your spouse's viewpoint. She will have a more objective understanding of the position of your coworkers on workplace subject matter. You may come to the realization that your lifelong companion is very intuitive when it comes to reading people and their subtle idiosyncrasies. This could include your own little nuances, which she handles on a daily basis without your knowledge. While she is listening intently to you, listen to her with the same intensity. Though you may be expecting her to solve your workday issues, keep in mind that, when she is discussing the angst and anguish of her day, she is not expecting you to fix anything. She just may be happy having a good listener, so be a good listener, and if she desires help, she will ask.

Be mindful of the fact that, if you are merely pretending to listen, you're busted. Don't believe she cannot detect your lack of interest. Remember communication is the most important aspect of any relationship. Without effective mutual communication, there is *no* relationship. You do not know her desires and she does not know your desires. *Wait, she does know your desires. She also knows you are not listening either, so good luck on the rest of the evening.*

You might take a nice after-dinner stroll through the park as you hold her hand *(provided you did not blow it at dinner).*

Also, when you get home from that relaxing evening, remember to start reducing that next-day stress and prepare for your Thursday. We live in such a fast-paced world these days, we should all do our part to slow things down a little. People often say they don't have time to do the things they enjoy. Usually this means they are not willing to take the time to do the things they enjoy. It is easier to wallow in self-pity than to actually do something about it.

Chapter 11

Thursday

(Another quiet evening out for dinner, and this time dancing.)

If you have been doing your part thus far, her stress level is most likely very low. Yours is, too. When stress is low, a relationship has the freedom to fly. *You may be surprised at the affection she begins to show you or the affection she's always had, and you are just now beginning to notice.*

Thursday is quite possibly the best day of the week. Why? Because, if you have weekend plans, you might have the opportunity to add Friday and Thursday magically becomes your Friday. Thursday also means let's get everything cleaned up today and maybe, just maybe, we can get out of here early Friday or at least on time.

If you do have weekend plans and you don't have an opportunity to forego Friday, check those reservations you made and make sure everything is a go. Naturally, if you will be taking Friday off from work, it would have been nice to do this on Wednesday, but take it in stride and don't cause any unnecessary stress. If you allow stress to take over, it will, so don't let late changes disrupt the flow, so that nice romantic weekend won't be ruined. If you do add Friday to your weekend, get those changes done early in the day on Thursday. In many cases, late changes are prohibited. If so, remember to plan early the next time. By checking on those reservations early, you circumvent the possibility that you could lose the reservations. *Hey, it happens!* Waiting until arrival to find your reservations were sent by a slow mole makes for unnecessary scrambling, while you are telling yourself, *"I should have checked, I should have checked."*

Finding out your plans have been mishandled is no cause for great concern, because it's Thursday, and you remembered to check that calendar daily, so you can head off any issues. Besides, if you are forced to change a location, maybe you find yourselves at new place that has even better accommodations!

Keeping on top of everything helps make your weekend go smoothly. You don't want a stressful weekend as, for most of us, the workplace fills that bill nicely.

If you are going to stay home and enjoy a relaxing weekend around the house, Thursday is a good night to go out for dinner and dancing. You're almost through the week, and it's time to shake it off and get ready to let the weekend roll. Starting to celebrate on Thursday helps Friday go well, and you will be amazed how an evening of dancing will invigorate your soul. Not to mention you get to spend some quality time with your best friend, companion and lover, with endless opportunities to tell her how much you love her. As you hold her and gaze into her eyes, what do you see? *Pure Heaven!* There is no better place to see deep into her eyes than when you are on the dance floor. Dancing washes away all stress and turmoil.

When you get home, you will be so relaxed, you may decide to bypass everything and lock up and retreat behind those closed doors. If you happen to have little ones, you will need to pick them up from the babysitter, get them ready for bed, and then you can make your retreat (hopefully). If not, there is always tomorrow and the evening out was nice. After all, the wee ones deserve your time, too. It's part of being that *Real Dad*.

Chapter 12

Friday

(Quiet evening.... #%@&#^#&.... again?
Okay, you cook, then go dancing!)

As the song goes, *It's Finally Friday!* Hopefully you will be off on a gloriously romantic weekend and you have already left town. Either way, Friday's are a special day. Special, since you reflect on the past week and revel about the weekend ahead. Special, for if you are not leaving town, you can give her an unexpected treat, just when she may be contemplating a dull evening at home. Go ahead. Make your regular morning call, but this time wait until the afternoon call to spring the surprise. I know. I said let her know early to maybe ease her day, yet sometimes it's nice to mix it up a little so she will be surprised because you waited until the afternoon call to tell her. This time call her a little earlier than usual, say shortly after lunch. She won't be expecting the call and you want to let the surprise have time to grow. Call her later in the afternoon and give her a few more tidbits of information about the evening you have planned, to add a touch more intrigue.

You have been out a few times this week and it was expensive, so dinner out is not the answer. How about dinner at home, cooked by you, with candlelight, soft music and flowers?

Leave work early if necessary to get everything prepared early, and clean up your mess. If she gets home before you, tell her to take a bubble bath while you finish up. You can tell her this will be somewhat of a formal dinner and she should dress for a romantic evening as it will be only the two of you.

What? You can't cook? That's a good excuse for the *"I will forever be dependent on someone else"* crowd. Basic cooking, and even more than basic cooking, can be learned by anyone. Besides, you don't have to produce an award-winning French cuisine meal. Just a great dinner for the one you love.

She will be receptive of whatever you have prepared. It's not just the food that makes the dinner. The ambiance and company make a difference as well. *Hotdogs won't do,* but there are plenty of foods you can prepare. After all, you are making these preparations for the loveliest, most beautiful woman on the planet. She will see you did all this for her and that you thought enough about her to do this. She will most likely be very appreciative of your efforts. Who knows? She may have her own surprise tucked away for a special occasion.

Are there other things you can do on Friday? Well, let's see. We've been through Sunday, Monday, Tuesday, Wednesday and Thursday, and it should be soaking in a little by now. Maybe you're one of those dependent people and need to be told what to do next. Better call your Mom and say, "Hi! Thanks for taking care of me." Then ask your spouse or significant other what she would like to do on Friday evening or for the weekend. *Chances are she already knows you don't have a clue.*

Chapter 13

Saturday

(Be creative: theater, beach, park, maybe a movie.)

    Things are warming up nicely for the weekend, we are in high gear, and stuff is happening. You might be away on that special weekend. Heck, just away for the weekend is good, or you may be at home. You can still be enjoying life to its fullest.

    Saturday is a great day for a nice surprise. Yep, out of the blue, totally and completely unexpected. You've had it planned for a couple of days and are waiting for the perfect time to spring your surprise. She may be expecting to stay around the house and do some much-needed yard work, clean out the closet, clean out the pantry, clean out the refrigerator, clean out the garage, clean out the....

    "*Whoa! Hold it!*" With all this cleaning, you would think you never did anything during the week or you are the most unorganized person of the century. But not for long, *right*? Because you have a plan!

    So, what do you do? Stop this madness and get that cleaning and boring stuff done during the week. The weekend is for fun, not work. You may say to her, "Let's go to a movie." Or "How about that new play at the local theater? The beach? How about shopping?

Or we could build that backyard swing you have been wanting?" Think of anything you know she might not be expecting and, flash, *there's the sparkle-in-her-eyes* instant surprise. She will love it, and you get the experience of seeing her joy. You are not the only one capable of spinning a surprise. Who knows, she may say, "Let's go play golf" or "Let's check out those new cars." You never know. That's why surprises are pleasurable and delightful.

Going to the local playhouse gives her a chance to dress up and forget about the stress of the past week. Maybe you attend an opera or ballet, both equally romantic and pleasing for both of you. I can think of nothing more pleasing than escorting a beautiful woman to the theater. Why? Because I get to sit beside her, hold her hand, look into her eyes and tell her how much she means to me and how much I enjoy being with her. Talk about the stress of the past week melting away! *What week? What day? I don't care. Just don't let this moment end too soon.*

Saturdays may seem to last only an hour or so when you are immersed in play, or Saturdays can last forever if you allow doldrums to control your day.

You may have kid things that don't allow for much free time, but if you really want to, you can find time. The kids will enjoy many things you do mostly because they are spending time with Mom and Dad. Saturday is like any other day. It requires some planning and forethought to ensure you don't waste away one of your two weekend days.

Saturday night is the pinnacle of the week. If you plan just right, schedule everything just so, Saturday night is the cat's meow. Nothing is off limits; nothing is out of reach. You need only to reach, and the possibilities are endless. For example, plan a different activity every Saturday. Remember: get creative. It is of no consequence what you do, where you do it, or how you do it, but the *when* is *Saturday*.

Go somewhere different, do something different, try new foods, try new things, anything. Swimming, diving, snorkeling, golfing, running, race car driving, skydiving, water skiing, snow skiing, walking, cooking sushi — oops! —*making* sushi, cooking, stomping grapes for wine, cattle driving, running of the bulls, playing tennis, watching tennis, playing softball, bowling, painting a picture, singing, star gazing, mountain climbing, watching people, rocket launching. Pick something, anything you have not done before, something invigorating. Challenge yourself; it will be fun!

If you don't like a chosen activity, fine. Then don't do it again, but as Mom says, "You won't know until you try it." So at least you tried it once.

Saturday is not the only day you can try new things, but it does offer you ample time to visit the emergency room should the need arise. *Although I don't know anyone who, by watching tennis or star gazing, was required to make a hospital visit for injuries sustained in those activities.*

Here's a safe idea if you're with friends: start a discussion about the strangest accident that happened during some activity you have done or seen. Surely, if you are prone to accidents, this discussion will be safe, unless you feel the need to demonstrate.

Back to trying something new. Sooner or later, hopefully much later, you will run out of new things to try. It could be because you are exhausted, or perhaps you live in a small town with not much to do. At the very least, while searching and trying new activities, you had the opportunity to enjoy those experiences with the love of your life. New experiences spark new feelings, new thoughts, and new ideas. You may be water skiing one day, as you fly into the air over that nasty wake, and suddenly you have just solved a puzzling problem you have been mulling over at work.

Not because your problem has to do with water, water skiing or any other activity you've engaged in, but because you have allowed your mind to be free and to wander. *(Of course, flying through the air on water skis may require some concentration, too.)* We often close our minds to anything new and simply plod through life doing the same thing the same way every day. Sometimes we complain, yet we still continue to slog along. Engaging in different activities and learning new things opens the door to a richer more abundant life.

Through happenstance, we may stumble across someone or someplace that appeals to us. We may also appeal to that someone or someplace and, just like that, magic happens in some of the strangest places. How do you think new products, new foods or new processes are invented?

Someplace, someone who was water skiing while testing a new ski design for their company one day, decided a nice snug life jacket was in order, probably shortly after colliding with the water.

Saturday is for romance. If Saturday provides us with time for new experiences, Saturday also allows us time for unencumbered romance. Just as the passage of time robs us of our days on earth, lost opportunities of romance are forever gone. As we travel on our journey of life, we encounter many opportunities. Some we embrace, some we pass, but without love, there is no life, and without life, no opportunity. Near the end of one's journey, I daresay not one person has ever said, "I wish I would have loved less."

Saturday is your last opportunity of the week to show your life's companion how much she means to you. If you have been listening, you are already aware of the possibilities. Remember our talk about listening? *Don't worry, we'll talk more.* Being a good listener is a very important character trait. If you don't believe listening is important, try this. When you get up on Saturday morning, pull on those jeans and head out to the hardware store or wherever you go on Saturday morning. Then go directly to a florist and pick up her favorite flowers. *You know where the florist is and what her favorite flowers are, because you have been listening, right?* Go back home, take those flowers inside, give them to her, and say, "Do you know how much I love you, how beautiful you are, how much I want to sweep you off to a place far away? A place where we can be alone, we can dream until day turns to night. Where the birds sing, and time stands still."

Her answer will be, *"What are we waiting for?"*

Chapter 14

New Year's Eve

(Dress up; make it romantic.)

The very first holiday of the year, this one will take some planning to get it right. Nearly every woman wants to go out on New Year's Eve. Thanksgiving and Christmas holidays are over, and all that stress has been building—not too much, however, if you have done your part along the way. Still, there will be some residual stress. A chance to relieve that stress will be graciously welcomed.

Pick somewhere that provides a soft candlelight dinner or at the very least low lighting with an atmosphere to create a perfectly incredible evening. The best plans would include an overnight stay after the midnight party is over. Let her know in advance that you are planning the evening out. Maybe right before Christmas or immediately after will help reduce holiday stress. Insist she shop for a new dress, shoes and purse for this evening of dinner and dancing. She will most likely need two pairs of shoes, one for dinner and one for dancing. You don't want painful feet to spoil a great evening for the both of you. Be especially mindful that, after the evening festivities are over and you're back in your nice comfortable room, an offer to rub her feet while adding some soothing lotion will be well received.

Go shopping with her to pick out her new clothes. She will want your input on just the right outfit. Be sure to let her know where you plan to take her and what the appropriate dress will be. Depending on your dinner location, it may be apropos for two outfits: one for dining and one for dancing. For the most part, you can usually find one suitable for both events, as changing clothes in mid-evening may be undesirable. Though, she will definitely need two pairs of shoes. She will be extremely appreciative that you realize her need for the second pair of shoes. *Don't be a jerk! Go to the car, get the shoes, and then return the other pair to the car.*

Dinner, yes. A quiet luxurious location to start the evening right and making sure her every desire is met certainly sets the tone for a wonderful evening. You want to show her off in her new dress; therefore, plan to enjoy a long slow meal, engaging in light conversation, and remember your manners. Talk with her, and her alone, as if no one else in the restaurant exists. She is watching to see if you are interested in her. Besides, you may be surprised to see how her eyes shine in the candlelight.

I suggest a glass of wine with dinner. The champagne comes later, if you prefer neither, that will be fine as well. You may toast the New Year in any way that is appropriate for you.

This would be a great time to give her a small gift—something from your heart to hers. A gift to tell her she is always the one and tonight begins anew, new experiences, new places and your continued love of her.

Party locations should be agreeable to both of you, but be cognizant of the number of people, what type of revelers may be attending, and whether it is indoor or outdoor. You don't want to be crushed while trying to dance or packed in your seats with 5,000 of your not-so-close friends. Loud, obnoxious, sloppy partiers can dampen the evening.

If the festivities will be outside, insure you have blankets, chairs, coats, jackets, gloves, umbrellas or anything you may need to brave the elements. Being cold, wet or standing all evening ruins a great time for everyone.

If the evening begins to wear on and it is not quite midnight, don't force her to stay. You can toast the New Year behind the privacy of those *closed doors.*

Chapter 15

Valentine's Day

(Dress up, romance, gifts and flowers.)

This is probably the most advertised day of all holidays, other than Christmas. No one usually forgets Valentine's Day unless stranded on a deserted island without a calendar and providing they know what day it was when they arrived on the island. Most men do a bang-up job of getting absolutely the wrong gift. Here is a tip, two words: *No lingerie.* Nada, not ever, never. If you want your companion to have or wear some sexy number for you, the best way to make that happen is: (1) read this book, do half of the suggestions you read here and you most likely you won't need to worry about such things, or (2) simply ask her. Do not go buy some "whatever thing" for Valentine's Day or any occasion.

It's not like she doesn't already know your thoughts. If you approach the situation properly, she may go make an appropriate sane purchase of lingerie herself and surprise you. The way to make your tastes known is to go with her when she buys these items. She will ask your opinion and will appreciate your shopping with her, too. You will be purchasing lingerie that she will be pleased to wear for you and, most importantly, clothing *she* likes!

Please save everyone's dignity by not going to a lingerie store shopping and discussing intimate apparel with some saleswoman whom you wouldn't recognize two minutes after you leave the store. All the while the saleswoman knows your companion will probably not like what you have picked out, but after all she most likely works on commission. So, don't blame her when your insensitivity falls flat. Then you bring this *little number* home and present it to her, and she is supposed to believe this a great gift of your love. *Yeah, right!!!!*

If you somehow could hear the words in her head at this exact moment, you may be appalled at what you hear. Fortunately, being the loving, caring person she is, she will likely not make a big deal of it and will graciously let you off the hook. *You may get to see her wear it ONE time, if you were smart enough to get the correct size.*

Valentine's Day is about romance. When is there a better time to tell her you love her than on Valentine's Day? The opportunities are endless. Commercially there are thousands of gift suggestions; you don't even have to be that creative.

Retail has done it all for you; delivery is up to you and deliver you should. And remember, don't wait for special occasions like Valentine's Day to say, "I love you." Tell her every day, show her every day, and be there for her every day. If you have ever said to yourself, *"She should be there for me,"* just look around. She *is* there for you, at home, at work, at play. She feels for you when you're down and *does for you every day.* Valentine's Day is a perfect opportunity to return her dedication, devotion and love in support of you. You did something in the beginning to give her cause to love and support you. So, I ask, *"Why did you stop? She didn't."*

Should you get her a gift? Yes, she should receive a gift for Valentine's Day. *Hey, you were willing to run out and buy that lingerie.* There are plenty of other items to adorn your shopping list. Obviously, candy, and it must be chocolate unless there happens to be some allergy prohibiting such. If you ask 100 women what they want for Valentine's Day, probably 80 or more will say *chocolate.*

Gifts can range from A to Z. Jewelry is nice. Gift certificates for shopping, dinner, dancing or day spas are also nice.

If I were asked to guess, I would say jewelry, chocolate and flowers are tops on the list.

This is not the time to point out your greatness because you got her two gifts, jewelry and chocolate, *and the chocolate was probably from the grocery store!* She deserves more, and if you expect to receive any gifts from her, don't be cheap. She will know if your gifts come from the heart, regardless of your gift. *(Well, not the lingerie, of course.)*

Flowers also. Never ever fail to buy her flowers on Valentine's Day. If she works, then have them delivered to work. I have them delivered a day or two before to avoid the rush, and she gets to be the first one in the office to receive flowers. Sending flowers is an easy thing to do, and she will love you for the gesture. I also go to the florist on Valentine's Day to purchase flowers, put them in her car, or take them home for her to find later.

Later we will discuss how flowers can be a great initiative for those *"I just wanted to surprise you"* occasions. Your gift of flowers does not necessarily have to be roses or even cut flowers. You can send potted flowers, and virtually any type of flower arrangement is acceptable.

Always send a card with those flowers and don't be afraid to tell the person on the other end of the phone what you want to say on the card. *They won't be embarrassed, though maybe slightly envious, hoping they receive the same consideration from their relationship.* Florists have an array of add-ons for floral arrangements. Visiting the florist will give you an idea of what is available. It's not a bad place to go. Get there, stroll on in, and look around. Florists are friendly people and will be happy to help. By looking at what is available, if you decide to call in your order later, you will know what you can add on to your order. Do not send the exact same thing every time. Mix it up a little, as you want her to be pleased and surprised.

If you are going to give her early warning about what the plans are going to be for her Valentine's night out, here is a good way to deliver your news. Tell her that both of you need to go shopping after work. She will ask why. You can let her know you're taking her out for Valentine's Day, and you thought she may want to get a new dress and such to wear for the evening.

If you choose to go out for the evening, take her dancing. *Remember we have already discussed this earlier.* This the absolute best time for you to look deeply into her eyes and see that beautiful shine. You are close, you get to hold her, and she will look radiant in her new dress. Dancing is the only time in a public setting with people all around that you can get very close, very personal, and it is acceptable behavior. On a dance floor, the sincerest, most endearing, most loving, and most meaningful feelings ever articulated are never verbalized.

Treat her with the respect she deserves and *you may find her urging you to retire a little early*. With all the people and dancing, those closed doors may be beckoning for a chance at some privacy. Remember her passion is fueled by the way you treat her, not by your lust.

Chapter 16

St. Patrick's Day

(Wearing of the green, Luck of the Irish. She will enjoy the surprise.)

It's St. Paddy's Day and spring is in the air. Life begins to renew and, depending on life's circumstances, it may have been awhile since she had an evening out. If you do not celebrate St Patrick's Day, that is fine, too. You can you use the day for an excuse to surprise her and celebrate the surprise.

This should be a "let's get together with a bunch of friends and rock the house." It's spring. Shake off the winter and start thinking about the beach. Find an Irish Pub and let the good times roll. If you don't happen to have an Irish Pub close by, then any good-natured establishment will do and many of them will have green beer for the occasion. Make it an after-work affair and, if she works, be sure to pick her up so she won't have to drive later. It gives her a chance to change into more casual clothes and she will appreciate the chance to relax on the way home after a night of fun and frolic. Remember to mind your manners, and don't be the *life of the party*. Leave that honor for someone else.

If you don't celebrate this occasion, then it is a good time to have an after-work happy hour or a get-together coffee meeting with friends. I like to fill those empty days when there is a distinct shortage of holidays and have after-work parties for a couple of hours.

You lose some of the stress of the day, you can talk about how lousy management is handling the latest crisis, kids, or the weather if you have nothing else to discuss. Often long-time mutual friendships are made from such occasions. You find out someone in your office enjoys sailing, hiking, rafting, skydiving or, for the really adventurous, maybe bowling.

When people move from one environment to another, they tend to speak more freely and, since you have very good listening skills now, you'll learn from others and enjoy the company.

When you attend these outings, be it St. Paddy's day or just an office get together, don't ignore your companion. But, don't smother her either. This does not mean to forget you have a companion. Mingle and allow her to mingle as well. She needs time to discuss her issues with her friends and you need the same.

Touch base occasionally. Maybe she is ready to leave or just wants to discuss something with you. Do not force her to overstay her limits. What are her limits? *Try asking.*

Chapter 17

Easter

(How about a new dress and maybe a drive in the country?)

Be sure to plan this a week or two in advance of Easter Sunday. The reason for this is she needs enough time to go shopping for a new outfit. Yes, you must go shopping with her. After all, she does value your opinion on what she wears. You may be thinking at this point that every occasion, holiday, vacation or happy hour is a requirement for new clothes. *Well, yeah it is, and you should embrace the opportunity for the time together*! No, you won't need to remodel the house and build bigger closets (unless you have small closets in the first place, then you probably already have plans for a remodel). She will cycle out the old to make room for the new. Besides, you want her to have new clothes so she looks nice. If you go shopping with her on a regular basis, there is no doubt that she will let you off the hook occasionally *if you just ask*. Don't take advantage of her, however, and start finding excuses for not going with her. Let her know you enjoy going shopping with her. Sometimes she may want to go by herself or with friends.

Plan for an Easter lunch after church. Maybe your family or friends have planned something. If not church, plan a special outing with family and friends. Maybe a drive in the country, or to the beach, or something. The reason for planning a lunch or an outing is for her to be able to wear her new outfit someplace other than just to church. Not to say this alone would not be enough, but it is nice to do a little extra. *Relax and enjoy the day.*

Chapter 18

Memorial Day

(Beach, beach, beach! Ok, ok, get away for the weekend somewhere.)

Several months have passed since we planned any real holiday time. Personally, I would have sneaked in a couple of three-day weekends by now, but if you prefer, you can wait for the arrival of this holiday. Don't be surprised if she mentions that some friends went out of town for the weekend a few weeks ago. She is trying to kick start your memory and remind you she would have enjoyed a weekend away, too. For the first typical long holiday weekend of the summer, it needs to be a fun place and a fun time. Spring has been around for a while now, and we are itching to get going, *somewhere!*

Before you ask, yes, she will need some new clothes, a new swim suit, shoes, maybe a hat or two, and possibly some new bags, depending on where your plans will be taking you.

Don't plan to go the same place you went last year. If you have built a family tradition of going to the same place every year, then more power to you. I much prefer to find new places, see new things, do new things, and visit with new people. I know you can be limited to your distance on a three-day weekend but, hey, you could extend it a day.

Ask her where she would like to go even if you do have some traditional locked-in-concrete can't-go-anywhere-else location. There is the possibility that it's time for a change. While you are thinking she is one that wants to keep doing the same thing, she may be thinking you are the drab "do the same thing forever" person. Ask her. It all goes back to that communication thing. Who knows? You may start a whole new family tradition. If you travel with friends every year, explore the off chance that they would like to try something new. Once again, as amazing at it seems, circumstances can change. Many times, we get set in a real rut and do the same thing over and over because *that's what we always do*. Reach out, touch another world; life exists outside your small comfortable circle.

If you want to have a nice long romantic weekend, maybe four or five days, Memorial Day is a great holiday for doing that. You can get out in the evening. It's warm, the weather is usually very accommodating, and you have no idea where a nice leisurely stroll in the moonlight will take you. Have you looked into her eyes in the moonlight? *Probably not since before you were married, if you even did it then!* Remember, "*LOVE is a many splendored thing*" and, believe it or not, love makes the world go around.

Unfortunately, many women in the world work hard to find even the smallest semblance of romance in their lives—and those are the married ones.

If you are one of the few that truly are romantic, you should not mind showing your intentions to the world. Let the world know; maybe they will learn from your actions. Don't be afraid to show affection; it's catching. Try it and you will see!

This first spring holiday of the year makes everyone excited to get outside and enjoy the warming weather. That is why I say, "Try something new." If you go someplace new every Memorial Day, the excitement surrounding this holiday will build with every approaching moment. Excitement is a good thing. You lose stress and you spend time planning with your companion and, by now you should know, any time you spend with your companion is time well spent.

You can visit travel agencies or you can visit travel websites. The website thing is kind of boring, but it works. Getting and reading the brochures printed by each exotic location is invigorating, as you read about all the amenities and activities. Talk about stress relieving! You may find that reading and discussing each location with your companion begins to transport you to the location and, before you know it, relaxation sets in and you feel like you are on vacation before you even leave home. Dreams do come true, especially when you are both at home feeling relaxed while dreaming about that heavenly romantic trip. *Sometimes you can take that trip and never leave home.* Eventually you have to come down from this euphoria and actually make the plans, but the road to getting there just got a little shorter and a whole lot easier. When you finally arrive at your chosen destination, you will always remember your previous *dream visit.*

Chapter 19

June Getaway

(Make one up, a three- maybe four-day weekend.)

This is a new holiday brought about by an ever-increasing sentiment of *let's get out of here this weekend*. Maybe you did not go anywhere for the Memorial Day holiday. In that case, shame on you, as we only have one Memorial Day per year and you missed it. *I hope there is a very good explanation*. My guess is you were given plenty of hints along the way. *See, your listening skills need more fine tuning*. Oh, by the way, you also missed that *dream visit*, too.

You have a chance to make it up to her with *June Day*. Even if you did go somewhere on Memorial Day, you should also plan for this event as well. I suggest you make this one a surprise.

You already know where her favorite places are. So you know what would make her day? Yep! A surprise trip! Plan it all and be sure to find out if she has any plans. You don't want to collide with work, travel or meetings that cannot be rescheduled. You can find a way to ask without giving away the surprise. Make all the plans and then let her know a couple of weeks or so in advance when and where you are going. *Yes, she will need time to go shopping.*

You can spring the surprise only a few days before, but let her know in time so she can get a few things for the trip. Your plan is to have an enjoyable relaxing weekend. Don't start off by waiting until Friday afternoon or Saturday morning to let her know you are going out of town for the weekend. Relaxing *it won't be* if you wait until the last minute. It would be like your boss telling you about a big meeting that requires a suit and tie five minutes before the meeting is scheduled to begin. You are to be presenting, and you have only come into the office to pick up a couple of things because you are technically off that day.

Remember to go shopping with her. She may want to ask questions about what you're doing, what the weather is going to be like, and will you be going out in the evening while on the trip? She will need this or that depending on the array of activities available at your new exciting romantic destination. It is simple. Get comfortable with the concept that she is more organized than you ever will be. Unfortunately, she can't plan her own surprise. So, the least you can do is give her time to acquire the things she will need and remember she will be getting what you need for the trip as well. *Because, you most likely never thought of that.*

Let her know if there may be dancing, as shoes are very important and, because she has shoes for the beach, shopping, dining out or casual wear, that does not mean any of those are appropriate for dancing. It is a fact, so there is no reason to argue about shoes.

Would you prefer she wear rabbit-ear house shoes? If this is your choice, then start over from the beginning of this book and read it this time. If she needs new shoes, buy her new shoes. If she wants new shoes, buy her new shoes. Go with her and let her know if you like the shoes she is selecting. *Unlike you, she will listen.*

I simply love surprise trips or weekend outings. I can never seem to get enough of them in during the year, but the look in her eyes and the smile on her face when I let her know we are going away for the weekend are the very reasons I strive to arrange as many as possible. A simple out-of-town weekend away from work and from the daily drudge makes all the difference in the world for creating peace of mind and showing her how much you love her.

I know you may be saying to yourself right now, *"If you do this all the time, won't it get boring and then there will be no surprises?"* Not if you go different places, do different things, and she doesn't know when you are going to plan a weekend away. That's why it is a surprise. She may be having a bad day or a bad week, and of course you should be communicating with her, but she still does not know when you are going to say, "Surprise!"

Some of my fondest memories are when I decided to send flowers and then, at lunch or after work, I would say, "Let's go so-in-so this weekend." Her eyes would light up, she would smile, and right then I told myself, *"Life is good when you share."* She knows I love her and I know she loves me. If I tell her on Monday afternoon about the weekend getaway, it may help relieve some stress and maybe make the rest of her week go a little better.

You don't necessarily have to go for the whole weekend. You can go for the day on Saturday or on Sunday afternoon. A day trip can be exhilarating, too. Again, someplace new can make all the difference. Exploring new places together is exciting, rewarding, and fun.

Chapter 20

July 4th

(Another four-day weekend, so enjoy the summer. It's already half over.)

It is virtually the middle of a glorious summer, and *you were going to perhaps waste it away at home?* I know, sometimes this holiday is in the middle of the week, but nothing says you can't celebrate it on the weekend before or after. I like to enjoy my July 4th weekend by adding on a few more days. What the heck! It's just vacation time. When this holiday is on Wednesday, which means four, maybe five, days extra for my weekend! I always add at least one day. If it is already a three-day weekend by my work holiday schedule, I can take one vacation day and make it a four-day weekend. Like I said, it is the middle of the summer. I might plan my annual vacation around this holiday, or maybe I'll take the extra time anyway and not interfere with my vacation plans. Whichever way you plan this holiday, be sure you find the most fabulous fireworks, a fitting end to a great weekend.

School is out and the kids are probably restless. They want to get out of town, and it's a nice break from work for you and the love of your life. Remember the sunscreen, plan lots of activities, and enjoy it like there is no tomorrow. After all, we are never promised even the next minute of our lives.

This is a true American holiday and we should celebrate it like Americans—have lots of fun, *spend a lot*, party a lot, and remember to call Mom just to say, *"Hi, Mom, we wanted to call and say Hi."* Hey, you can never tell your Mom too many times that you love her.

Begin planning for this holiday early to ensure everyone is on board and has the opportunity to make appropriate schedule changes.

Let's get back to why we are here. This holiday is a happy time for all, and it should be a happy time for your significant other as well. Don't head off to the sports store, boat place or wherever and leave all the details to her. She may want to go along and you both can plan together while you are shopping.

This is probably a good time for me to say, "If you want separate holidays and vacations, then find another book. Sadly, this one is definitely not for you." You are halfway through this book and you still don't have a clue. *Typical.*

Check out Chapter 32 on *Afterthoughts.* Maybe you will begin to understand. This chapter will help you regardless of your personal female and romantic situations. Yes, I know that sometimes a little bit of alone time is good. This alone time is also something you should plan for together. Then you and she will know it is "alone" time—a time you both understand is a necessary time and not a time of frustration because you may think the other is not speaking for some unknown reason.

Now, enough of this down stuff. If you have been listening to her and communicating with her, then this "alone" thing will never be an issue. It will happen when it should happen.

Back to planning our big blowout weekend. Find out where she would like to go, let her know where you would like to go, and ask the kids, too.

I find it helpful on all holidays and vacations to make a checklist. It saves me from my ever-increasing forgetfulness, something we all suffer from at times. This checklist is a reminder about when to make reservations and the sort. She will be appreciative of your taking the lead role in making the plans. Discussing the plans with her along the way insures you will have a great time and serves as a mediator when those best-laid plans begin to unravel as oftentimes they do. Don't over plan things to do, like in trying to fit ten days of activities into five days. I like to arrive back home early in the evening so I have plenty of time to unpack, unwind and rest up for work the next day. We might even come back a day early so we can mentally and physically prepare for our unassuming reentry into to the workplace.

Make sure you pack the car and the suitcases. *(Note: even if it means taking extra suitcases, insure you have packed everything she wants to take along. That list really helps here.)* Prepare the house for your absence and, most of all, prepare the house for your return. For example, you do have to return and coming home to a "ready for the workday" house is very comforting and stress reducing (i.e., don't leave a mess when you leave). When you get home, don't destroy your "ready" house by filling it with the spoils for your trip. Unpack the car, unpack the suitcases, and unpack your purchases so your house and your life are restored to that nice serene "ready" state. How else would you be able to relax and rest up from your trip? In case you haven't noticed, one of the small themes throughout this book is *organization*, an important step to insuring your lives have a little less stress and a lot more time for more important things, like each other.

So, spice it up a little. Don't go to the same place every year. Exploration founded our country, so explore! It is indescribable how you feel when you have new experiences to enjoy with your life's companion. Even if one of you has previously visited a place, being there together for the first time is new and, well, *indescribable*.

There is a certain feeling deep down inside, and you know, as you look into her eyes and feel her touch, that you both have the same feeling and no one can ever take that moment away.

This is one reason I like to explore new places and, when we visit the old familiar places we love, it still feels incredibly warm and inviting. Each time we go out to dinner that feeling is there. Each time we look at the scenery that feeling is there. Each time we walk in the moonlight that feeling is there. Each time we touch, that feeling is there. Each time I hear her voice that feeling is there.

Chapter 21

August Last Hoorah

(A week just for the two of you; school starts soon!)

If your life includes a family, then take some time occasionally for just the two of you. Arrange whatever is necessary to get this time for both of you. Impose on relatives, call a friend or arrange summer camp; whatever it takes, do it. You know school will be starting soon and you should do whatever is necessary to get prepared early. Schools these days publish a required supplies list. Get it taken care of early to avoid the last-minute rush and that stress connected to the beginning of the school year.

Take the kids shopping after work. Don't rely on her to do everything while all you do is sit back and echo those stupid and heartless words, *"I'm paying for it. That should be enough."* It is August. We have been through a lot together in this book, and by now you should know that kind of attitude will get you nowhere, and we haven't even begun to talk about the holidays!

Cheer up! If you have been paying attention, you would not even consider uttering those words. Besides, if you have done even half the things in this book up to this point, she might even say to you,

"Honey, I will take the kids to get school supplies. You stay home and relax." And you know she really means it. As opposed to, "I will take the kids to get school supplies and we will *talk* later."

"August Day" is one of those surprise trips where you give her time to prepare. Don't tell her Friday afternoon that you two are going away for the week. While this late week announcement may be a surprise, it can well be an eye-opening surprise for you when her answer is a flat, *"No way, no how. I don't have anything prepared, and why didn't you tell me sooner?"* As we discussed, surprises are indeed surprises and have the same effect when you plan ahead. You receive the joy of surprising her, and she will be very receptive to the necessary lead time.

Yes, that is correct—you guessed it! Go shopping! You can plan the details for the kids ahead of time, and swear the relatives and the kids to secrecy. Think of a few different destinations and, when you let her know about the impending trip, offer two or three options. Then you both decide which location is the very best for your trip. After all, this is supposed to be a romantic time for you both of you, and it would be nice if she is pleased with the chosen destination. Romance is work, romance is fun, romance is easy, romance is exciting, romance is life, and romance happens when you least expect it. *Romance never happens when you attempt to control it.*

After you have chosen your location, begin planning your activities. Ok, I know this is supposed to be a surprise, but if you let her know early enough, it will be a much more exciting and fun-filled experience. Besides, you have already created a surprise since she had no idea you were planning anything.

Don't begin a slow backslide because you want to catch that special game or something else equally ridiculous. If situations arise and you need to pare back the time, of course you will both do what is necessary, but insure the circumstances require a shortened trip, *not because of selfishness on your part.*

She would have already told you during the early planning stages if a situation had existed that would cause the need to shorten the trip. *Don't make up empty meaningless excuses. She will see your reluctance and realize it is not only your excuses that are empty and meaningless.*

As with all long trips or long weekends, planning too many activities simply creates stress. Some of my most enjoyable and loving weekends were just the two of us hand in hand walking on the beach. I realize you may not want to walk on the beach endlessly for several days (to some this activity may be reprehensible, while others may find it delightful). My point is to make sure to plan your time accordingly and leave plenty of time for simply being together. Another of my very happy trips was an impromptu weekend where we planned no special activities. Each day we made it up as we went along. I know, I said you should plan. Well, we did plan. We planned to enjoy each new day and whatever that day brought to us. How do you say, *"Gloriously wonderful and exciting?"* That unplanned trip was a bona fide smorgasbord every evening with the air full of captivating charm as we discussed our next day's expedition.

Above all other times of the year—birthdays, anniversaries, Easter, Christmas and other holidays—this one miniscule mid-year trip gives you precious few hours alone with your soul mate. These treasured scant hours, compared to thousands upon thousands of hours in our lives, without question are the most important times in your relationship. This is the time she should be treated with loving charm. Treat her like what she is to you, a celebrity, her every wish embellished beyond belief, her every thought applauded, her very being favored again and again. *She deserves the best.* Pamper her with soft loving caring hands and words of affection. She has done for you, made for you, worked for you and gave to you her all, and she will continue to give and love you tirelessly.

This is her time. Treat her with respect, with love, and cherish these few hours, as they soon vanish like fog on a sunny day. It seems too often we find it very easy to say, "Next time." Too easily we forget we have no guarantees, and this may very well be the last time. *Are you going to chance losing it forever?*

Chapter 22

Labor Day

(Our last four-day weekend of the summer.)

Definitely plan this holiday as a four-day weekend, yet consider five, as it will be worth it. You may be asking, *"Haven't we had enough four-day weekends?"* My answer? Absolutely not! In my opinion, you should never go longer than 45 days without a three- or four-day weekend. As you may have noticed thus far, I advocate four days as opposed to three days at every opportunity.

It is only one more day and, if you do not want to spend that extra day out of town, then come back home and spend the extra day at home. *I promise* you will be more relaxed, less irritable, and have a better outlook on life by simply extending your holiday time and adding a few more long weekends throughout the year.

We spend too much time working and very little time living. Adding all the extra vacation days I am suggesting throughout the year comes to an additional 15 or so days away from your work. In total, approximately a month. I bet, if you try, you could talk yourself and your budget into a month off. By spreading it over the entire year, I am sure work won't miss the productivity. She will love you for it, your kids will love you for it, and *you* will love you for it. If you're one of those that take a regularly scheduled vacation each year, then bravo. A few extra days here and there won't do any harm. Who knows? Maybe your co-workers, supervisors, managers or employees would love to get you out of the office for few extra days. You won't miss the time either. A chance for some relaxing time away from work helps clear the mind. You might even find the solution to some perplexing problems while you're strolling along that beach or trying to stay awake as you float down that lazy river. *Careful, you may begin to realize it was a good idea to work out an extra month of vacation,* so don't make the Labor Day holiday laborious.

Since many of our lives are focused around school schedules, I see this holiday to be the last one of the summer season. Therefore, make it relaxing and enjoyable for all participants. Plan activities that everyone enjoys or plan activities aligned with each one's likes rather than dislikes. You truly can please everyone if you understand that everyone will be open to compromise if they get to participate in their favorite activity along the way. You don't want someone wishing they had stayed home or being unhappy because he or she failed to do something they wanted to do during the last summer outing of the year.

If your schedules are not affected by school, then plan on a relaxing, soothing and stress-free trip, because it's still the last big holiday of the summer. Whatever your interests and ambitions are, this is not the trip where you decide it's time to try skydiving, mountain climbing, cliff diving or some other equally dangerous feat. Beginning the early fall season wearing a fashionable cast or brace of some sort tends to get everyone off to a bad start, especially since you may be sporting these devices into the holiday season.

Yes, I know you could go snow skiing in November and befall a similar situation with being in a cast for the holidays, but if you like snow skiing or you are looking to learn this year for the first time, you don't want to be hampered by some late summer fling requiring extended and painful recuperation causing you to miss that big ski trip.

Aside from that, your undivided concentration is going to be needed to help her through the holidays beginning, with Thanksgiving. So, make Labor Day a weekend of fun for all, including you. *You deserve a fun time, too.*

Chapter 23

October Fest

*(Mountains, autumn leaves, quiet,
one more long weekend before the holidays.)*

October Fest, Fall Fest, whatever you call it, when those gray days of fall start showing up. Festive is a good thing. Remember, I recommend taking at least a three-day weekend every 45 days. Don't get picky now and grab a calendar to lay out a perfect schedule. The suggestion is not meant to be *exactly every 45 days on the dot.* You are supposed to be scheduling relaxation time, not increasing stress by having a penchant for specificity. Once you get in the swing of it, you won't even think twice and, strangely enough, you will likely be looking forward to the time off. *For once, a schedule everyone wants to keep.*

October is much like spring in many locales of our country, from the weather perspective of modest change to bold change. We discussed taking a weekend back in March, April or May, depending on where you live to enjoy spring in full bloom. Most every area has some sort of springtime festivities to celebrate the rejuvenation of life and nature. If you didn't take advantage of that opportunity back in the spring, then don't slip up here in October. Be sure you make amends here and resolve to do better beginning now.

And, by the way, if you did miss the spring trips, you are still not *listening*. We didn't specifically discuss spring, but we did discuss other ways to show her you are thinking about her. You know she would love a weekend outing to see flowers and gardens as the cascading colors appear. Strolling hand in hand through a botanical garden flowing with blooms of every variety does wonders for relaxation. Romance can bloom in the spring as well, especially if you have been thoughtful enough to find her a garden overflowing with beautiful flowers.

October offers as much finery in way of natural change as spring. However, in some locations of our country, October may be a bit late to view the changing leaves and landscape, so you may need to slide in a few days here and there before October.

October does spawn many fairs and festivals around the country and the leaves usually begin to change sometime during the month. So, get out your planning book, calendar, PDA or whatever you use to keep track of your life, and search for the perfect place to enjoy those beautiful autumn leaves.

Fairs and festivals offer much in the way of fun, entertainment, learning and excitement. Nearly every event has some local entertainment and, more often than not, the entertainment is excellent. Singing, dancing and eating are the usual fare, and most events schedule several different performances for the pleasure of all attendees. What is offered in the way of craft shows, festivals and fairs depends on your area of the country. I have visited events with demonstrations covering craft making, building furniture, making knives and even making horse drawn carriages.

A variety of goings on can be found at a fair or festival, and, in many areas, you can pick what type and flavor of event you want to attend. If festival hopping is not your cup of tea, then you can find parks, museums, nature walks or hiking trails in every state. Remember shopping though, a virtual necessity, and if you want to make her happy, taking time to shop on your trip will definitely be a favored activity.

This is one of those planned weekend trips that you know you are going to take, but I like to mix things up a bit and plan to go different places each year. You may need to add a day but, *hey, four days is always better than three.* It is easy to search the internet and find areas of fall foliage. If you are lazy, you can find them on The Weather Channel website.

Fall, like spring, is great for long walks day or night. In spring, you get the fresh air, the smell of blooming flowers, and long warm evenings. In fall, you have fresh crisp cool air and crystal-clear skies, *all the more reason to get a little closer*. I particularly like fall because I can get really close with my wife when riding in a horse drawn carriage in the evening. If you have never tried carriage rides, then *she deserves* an opportunity to have the experience.

If you're not the carriage type, then sailboats work well also. I like both methods of travel as they provide a somewhat quiet passage. In the case of sailboats, once you leave the pier area, all you hear is water and sails. In my humble opinion, probably the ultimate romantic evening in the spring or fall is a simple rowboat ride on a quiet little lake. As you lay back and hold her, you can hear the hushed sounds of life with the most glorious stars high above. You feel like you could reach out and touch them. Most often though, all I hear is a gentle heartbeat as I feel the soft touch of her hand in mine.

Chapter 24

Thanksgiving

(Keep her stress level to the absolute minimum. Help her out – a lot!)

For most of our cherished companions, November is the beginning of a very stressful holiday season even before Thanksgiving arrives. It means preparation, planning, working, working and more working. All this planning and working is just to arrive at Thanksgiving Day. To put it more simply, stress, stress, stress is the order of the day, and you can and should do as much as possible to relieve that stress. Her knowing you're there and are willing to help with every aspect of the hectic holiday season speaks volumes about your support of her. You can ease her stress even more by planning with her and taking as much of the tasks leading up to Thanksgiving Day off her calendar. *Can you do this? Of course, you can!* You are already helping by keeping the regular household events on schedule and, with a modest amount of communication, much of the holiday blues will fade away.

Let's start with a little planning. Are you going away for Thanksgiving or are you hosting family for Thanksgiving? If you are traveling, then the stress level is way down already. You both sit down at the beginning of the month and lay out a tentative schedule. Include Christmas as well since you're there, and it will help later to know your proposed plans in case they need to change as Christmas approaches. Any plans you make now can obviously be changed and likely will have minor modifications. However, you have a starting point and, with a single planning session, you are helping to reduce stress. Take care not to build a mental attachment to this schedule. If this schedule becomes the master of your life, it will only cause additional stress. *Be flexible.* All plans change; the trick is adjusting to the change.

Another stress reducer is accepting up front that you may be required to adjust the schedule. Now you are more relaxed because you have this starting point. It only takes a few minutes to add some Christmas plans at the end of your Thanksgiving *communications.*

So now you ask, "Heck, *why make plans at all if they're going to change anyway?"* An early holiday season schedule serves as a base point and both of you will be working from the same base point. This is vital to a successful holiday season. We've talked about communication, and this is the best practical application. If you can plan and work through changes in these two holidays, then the rest of the year is *daises.*

Here is a quick checklist to get you started:

- Holiday planning the first of November
- Office parties (If you know the dates, put them in your calendar.)
- Traveling:
    - Where? How long? Trip alone or to a family gathering?
    - Make reservations as early as possible.
    - Christmas shopping now; don't wait.
    - What dates do you plan for traveling?
    - Are you coming back early for rest time?
    - Make a list of what needs to go with you.
    - Schedule car maintenance if driving a long distance.
    - *Be on time.*

- Not Traveling:
    - Entertaining family or maybe friends
        - How many?
        - How long will they stay?
    - Complete food menus for snacks, dinner
    - Activities for kids and adults
    - Christmas shopping now; don't wait.
    - Furniture rearranging? Do it now, if practical.
    - Cooking supplies now
    - Who is cooking what? When?

- Who is bringing food? What are they bringing?
- *Be on time.*

These are just some of the items you may want on your list. *Make only one list.* It doesn't have to be maintained in a single place. You can both have a copy and do the updates every evening. Having this list and following this list will get you through the holidays all the way to midnight on New Year's Eve.

You may actually find it amusing that you are *making your list and checking it twice!* The existence of a safe haven, so to speak, is comforting and relaxing.

Be smart and make a copy of your much-altered list so you will have a good start on next year's holiday season planning.

Ok, you have decided you are staying home this Thanksgiving, so what's next? After you have finished your preliminary checklist, get started on a Christmas gift list. Keep them separate but close at hand. Go Christmas shopping anytime the opportunity avails itself. I know you would like to wait for all those new gadgets and toys that show up a few weeks before Christmas.

Also remember that most of the holiday ads are specifically designed to get you in the mood for some impulse buying. If you decide to wait for those last-minute sales, then be mindful to update that list as changes occur and keep *checking*. The best prices are early in the season and, quite frankly, the best quality as well. Some people like to start shopping early to spread out those expenses. Getting as much Christmas shopping done as soon as possible is a huge stress reliever for both of you.

While we are on the topic of shopping again, I remind you to go with her and help as much as possible. And she may be fine with your staying home with the kids and be very appreciative of your support. The important thing is to make sure you discuss (*communicate*) these things with her so you know where you can be the most help. Whatever your agreement, be sure to have a plan and, if that means getting out and going shopping with her, *then get with it!*

If you are one of those persons that accompanies your companion to the store and flops down on the nearest bench for the duration, then a few words come to mind: inconsiderate, rude, heartless, despicable and just plain selfish.

If this is your style, then your reading comprehension so far is much lower than you may think. *Although I am sure it is at a level your companion knows only too well.* Don't think for one second she is believing you are helping by driving her to the mall and then abandoning her while she does all the work. Hopefully, your comprehension is good enough for you to at least carry out the packages. If not, at this point, my guess is she would have preferred you had stayed home and out of her way.

Go with her and help her every step of the way. You have an influence on what is purchased when you are with her, and she appreciates your thoughts. You may know a person on the shopping list does not want what she has picked out. Communicating this knowledge to her translates into her not being embarrassed later when your family or friends open an "Oops, I already have one of those" gifts.

Also, you might actually have a good time while you're shopping with her!

Ok, enough on the Christmas shopping. Let's get back to our Thanksgiving festivities already!

Traveling

If you're traveling this holiday, make sure you check with your hosts about what you should bring along. For example: blankets, pillows, cots, sleeping bags, food, etc. If you are going to prepare *your special holiday dish* on site, be considerate and bring all the necessary ingredients with you. Don't expect your host to shop for you. Long trips need to be planned with ample stops along the way for rests and maybe a short walk. When arriving at your destination, you want everyone as relaxed and rested as possible. Arriving with tired and irritable passengers only serves to dampen everyone's holiday spirit. *(Hint: Make sure you are not irritable as well.)*

Be overly considerate of all participants and your holiday will be memorable as well as enjoyable. Be eager to help anywhere you may be of service. If you prefer to stay out of the resting-after-dinner group, then helping with everything is an excellent way to do so and the time will seem to pass much more quickly. I'm not saying you have the attitude of "getting out of there" but, in most situations, by the time Thanksgiving Dinner is served, everyone is fairly well talked out. Except for those few that may *never* be talked out. Everyone has something important to say and, as the host or a guest, you should be courteous and listen. *I'm sure they listened while you were telling your stories.*

As you are helping out, pay particular attention to your loved one. She needs you now very much. Check in often as she may need you to go get some supplies, she may need help moving things, she may want you to taste her special recipe, or maybe she just likes knowing you are close by and there for her.

Not Traveling

Your role is altogether different since you decided to stay home. You are the hosts and very soon much chaos will be at your door. Preparing for this event early rather than last minute will change a nightmare into pleasure as if by magic. We have discussed planning in advance and thankfully during the holidays it is much easier when we know early on whether we will be hosting and approximately how many are coming.

Get out your list. It may be time to begin making those changes. Put everything you can imagine on this list and even some things you would never imagine, like *"You ordered the turkey, but when you go to pick it up, it's not ready or there is no record of the order, or oops, the store made a mistake and gave your turkey to someone else."* It happens, so plan for it and life will reward you. Also add to the list the proposed number of guests, and keep track of special requirements like no salt, no spices, must have cornbread for your favorite aunt, etc. Believe me, a small amount of knowledge in these areas will reap seemingly gargantuan rewards in the form of peace and tranquility.

You have your list; now start working the list. I know it's the second of November, and you think you have plenty of time. Sure! *Now get the list out and let's get started!*

First, shopping. *Yes, and go with her!* Get those purchases out of the way, things such as paper goods, dishes, chairs, beds, decorations for the house, and take care of any entertainment or reservation requirements. Update your list and don't be afraid to add things along the way. Keep everything on the list even if you have completed the task. It feels good to visualize your actual progress. Also remember you are building a list for future use as well.

Now is a very good time to say to her, *"Hey, it is only the second of November. We have not had a weekend away for about a month or so. Why don't we go away this weekend, just the two of us? I will get on top of this list next week and if we have missed anything, we can discuss it. So, what do you say, shall we make it a weekend?"*

Even if the answer is, *"No, we can't. I have to be at so and so on Saturday"* you have set the tone for a more casual, less stressful holiday season. There's that surprise factor working wonders, and who knows? Maybe she can rearrange her schedule.

Weekend's over; now it's back to work.

Don't badger the relatives about what they are going to bring. Ask them to bring their favorite dish. *List time!* If they want to bring a specific dish, then add it to the list. Discuss it with them. Tell them they are not required to bring a dish, but it is appreciated (this is only for local guests). Some relatives will appreciate not being required to bring anything, as they would just like to visit, eat and relax.

Your main focus, as always, is your loving companion. Whether she is your wife or girlfriend, continually have her foremost in your mind. As the month grinds down, keep her informed of the progress on the list. It shouldn't be a problem because you both have access to the same list. *Communication, right?* Assure her you will be at her side. If she needs extra supplies, different supplies, a quick change in décor, or anything, she should know you are there to get it wrapped up.

During the busy holiday months, never abandon your love. Assure her you are only one touch away whenever or wherever she needs you. As you both venture through the holiday season hand in hand, there will be little that can dampen spirits and much to be thankful for as you rejoice in your happiness with each other.

Chapter 25

Christmas

(Give, give, give. Remember, your job is to keep her stress level low.)

I have kept Christmas separated from Thanksgiving (except for that gift shopping thing we talked about) as they are separate and distinct holidays with separate and distinct purposes. Christmas, with what it represents, is personal to each and every one of us. For me and my family, it is the celebration of the birth of Jesus Christ. Others may have different reasons to celebrate. Whatever your reason, there is still much opportunity for stress for everyone.

Christmas to me has always been a time for family, friends and love for all. Most of us are extra helpful and friendly during the holidays; some may ask why we are not helpful and friendly all year. *Well, my friend, that concept could and does fill volumes in many different forums.* Depression, anxiety, apprehension, fear and loneliness are all magnified during the holiday season. Any assistance offered to humankind, whether it's a holiday or any other day of the year, makes your heart beat a little bit stronger.

During the holidays, I endeavor to insure everyone I meet, greet, talk with, work with, love or even pass on the street, knows that I acknowledge his or her existence in our world. I want to let them know I am willing to converse with or assist them any way I can with all the physical and mental abilities afforded me. *Not just at Christmas but every day of the year.*

In my opinion, as we bustle through our daily lives and get caught up in the speed of our existence, we let too many things slide. So, I force myself to be mindful of this shortcoming during the holiday season and use it as reminder to continue this behavior throughout the year.

During Christmas, unlike Thanksgiving, everyone is a little more on edge, dealing with crowds of people and relatives. You don't know if people will like their gifts, you hope you haven't missed anyone, you have to go to the office party, you have to go to different friends' parties, you have guests coming for the holidays, or you have to travel for the holidays. You worry about all the costs; many people worry whether they can even afford gifts. All these things and more create stress and uneasy feelings for all of us.

"The list" is what keeps us on track during the holidays and the vehicle I use to insure I don't let anything fall through the cracks. As during the Thanksgiving holiday, I prepare for the event of traveling or not traveling.

I may add or change but I seldom delete from this list of activities. Sometimes the holidays are less stressful simply because you don't travel and you don't have family or friends over, but most of us still scurry about and find ourselves in stressful situations. Organization and communication help immensely with our shopping, decorating and socializing, but you can help reduce that stress by organizing and maintaining your list.

I look forward to visiting the malls on Friday after Thanksgiving. The hustle and bustle of all the people is exciting, and I enjoy watching everyone rush about visiting with friends, generally enjoying the season. Others I see may not be having such a great time, but that is because they don't have "The List".

Usually if I have kept on track with my list (every now and then, I find myself playing catch up), much of my Christmas shopping is complete, I don't have to rush about and endure long lines. Especially with all the online options available to us these days. Although I have been asked to go get a special gift at the eleventh hour. *Did I do it? Absolutely!*

Back to taking care of number one. *No, I don't mean yourself!* Ask her if she would like to go shopping so you can help her wrestle with the bags and endless lines of people. She may prefer you take the list and brave the masses. Trust me, it is not that difficult to go down a list and purchase those items—other than possibly encountering some less-than-friendly persons along the way. Meeting new people is fun and enjoyable, and you have an opportunity to brighten someone else's day—just by smiling and offering to help those less-than-friendly people. Even if you do offer to brave it alone, I am reasonably sure she will want to accompany you and be very pleased you offered to help.

If you don't already know what she wants for a Christmas gift, this is an excellent time to make some inquiries. Chances are, if you are observant, she will make subtle hints and suggestions as the day progresses. Let's hit on that communication thing again. She has been telling you for months now what she would like. All you had to do was *listen*. Your subtle inquiries now help to find out if she has changed her mind and has put something new on her list. These are stressful days for everyone, so don't be short with your answers and make sure you ask if she needs a rest or maybe suggest a long relaxing lunch.

Don't bulldoze through the list rushing around pushing everyone and everything aside with the false pretense of getting everything completed more quickly. It is time you learned that shopping is not simply going to one store, picking up one shirt, paying for it, and walking out. You may have a reason to purchase that shirt other than that *the one you are wearing is dirty*.

You may need a new shirt for a specific pair of pants. Does this one go with any other items you have in your closet? What other colors are available? That shirt over there will look nice with your gray trousers. Or you need some shoes for that upcoming business trip, etc. At the same time she is shopping for you, she is shopping for virtually every other member of the family.

Shopping cannot be rushed and, believe it or not, women can and do save money shopping. If you are going to do the bulldozer thing, then save her the trouble. Fall in line with the others who stay at home or wait on a bench somewhere while she does all the work. By the way, while you are lounging at home or sitting on that bench complaining to whomever may listen about the horrendous difficulties with holiday shopping; here are a few more things for you to think about.

Is your couch comfortable enough for sleeping on all night *(maybe several nights)*? Do you expect to eat when you get home and do you expect her to even talk to you for the next few days? As we have discussed thus far in this book, if she really is the love of your life, tell her, show her, do for her. After all, take note that, even with all of your complaining, she continues to do for you every minute of every day, even before you were married and only dating.

This brings us to that communication thing again, the part where she talks, and you don't listen. One of the most important things you can do in a relationship is listen. If you expect the relationship to last for any length of time, you must listen. I heard someone say, "I've been married twenty plus years and I don't have that problem." This statement is a strong testament to his wife and what she has endured for all those years and still tirelessly continues to "do" for him. With that attitude, he probably does not know exactly how many years they have been together anyway!

There is no greater gift at Christmas, or anytime for that matter, than giving. If I received absolutely no gifts during Christmas, as long I could give gifts and give of myself to make someone happy, I would consider my Christmas a tremendous joyful success.

Chapter 26

Her Birthday!

(Take off work. You do all the work. Give nice gifts and flowers.)

What? Only a day? How about the whole week! This is the only day of the entire year that is uniquely hers. She does not need to share it with anyone, although she will unselfishly share her day with family, friends and co-workers. Your task is to make sure she knows it is *her* day. If she works, encourage her to take the day off. Her co-workers can have their celebration before or after her birthday. They won't be upset if they know she is taking the day for herself. Family and other friends will want to celebrate her day, too; they won't mind a separate day either. Whatever day both of you pick as "the day" do whatever is necessary to insure this day is for her and her only. Plan to take the day off. Encourage her to do anything she desires, as there will be no tasks for her, no schedules, no work and no worries. Be her personal chauffeur and servant all day.

Wherever she wishes to go, wait for her. It could be she is getting her hair or nails done. Maybe she wants to spend the whole day at a spa. Encourage her; it is her day. Maybe she would like to sleep in, have a late breakfast, go out for breakfast, have an exotic lunch someplace special. Anything goes! No rules. Everything is a green light.

If you have been paying attention, you already know what she would like for her birthday. Remember flowers, flowers, gifts, gifts, flowers, gifts, flowers, gifts...*are you getting the picture?*

Flowers should be delivered at work before her birthday arrives. Let her co-workers see you care enough to send flowers even before her birthday. If she must be at work, send her some on her birthday, too! My goal for the day is simple: to shower her with her favorite pleasures so she will be so entranced the day will melt away. Birthday does not mean daytime only. There is a birthday night as well. She won't mind getting in late if both of you have planned a romantic dinner out. Don't just go off and plan in a vacuum. This is her day, so discuss it with her and let her make the choices. Go easy on the champagne, too. You don't want her to end her perfect day feeling miserably ill.

Another good plan is to let her know a few days ahead of time that you think the both of you should make her birthday celebration a whole week, weekend, or maybe a three-day weekend. It will be a surprise, but be sure to allow time to plan and go shopping. She can go to work and let her co-workers know you care enough that you are taking her on a trip for her birthday. Plan to return home fairly early from your trip. You want her to have plenty of time to unwind and relax. Remember, her birthday does not end until she goes back to work. Even if you return on Saturday, her birthday does not end until work time on Monday morning. It is her time. Let her enjoy it. Moreover, *make sure* she enjoys it.

The most unfeeling thing you can do is set up a celebration time and then, after this celebration time has passed, act as if the birthday is over. Unfortunately, too many men act unfeeling, uncaring and just plain rude, but they turn the tables when it's their birthday. All you hear is howling and whining, "It's *my* birthday!"

Ask some wives how many times they hear "*It's Father's Day. I am not going to do that,*" or "*Leave me alone; it's my birthday.*" Sometimes as I observe people going about life, I ask myself, "*Has our civilization advanced so very little from those days when women were considered property?*"

Back to HER birthday!

She may want to just take it easy around the house and be treated like royalty. If you have kids, make sure they also understand this is her day. If they need anything, they should be asking you, after all *you took the day off too just for this purpose.* Don't get busy with other things around the house or yard or find some excuse to leave. You need to be at *her beck and call.* She should be going back to work to tell her friends how lavishly she was treated on her birthday.

Back to the gift thing we discussed earlier. Sometimes several gifts are better than one. Get her something special for her to open on her birthday, but a little gift here and there before her birthday lets her know you never stop thinking about her. Multiple gifts are especially important a day or two prior to her birthday and even something small the day after her birthday when she is getting ready for work or preparing for the day. A gift will be a wonderful surprise to say to her that she is special and deserving.

(Hint, Hint: Gifting is a good idea throughout the year. You don't have to wait for her birthday.)

Chapter 27

Anniversary. No. Anniversaries!
(There are definitely more than one.)

You're married, and you think you have one anniversary—the date of your wedding day, correct? WRONG!! You're not married, and you think you don't have an anniversary to celebrate, right? WRONG!! For all men in any relationship, anniversaries include the day you first met, the day you started dating, and dates of any plans you have made for future anniversaries. For example, the day of your engagement, the day you set the wedding date, the day you proposed to her, and your wedding day—all these dates are important and should never be considered unimportant. These dates will always mean something to both of you. Even if she has trouble remembering other things (*although not very likely, as who takes care of you?*), she will remember these dates.

You certainly should remember these dates as well. If you have trouble remembering things, then these events go on your perpetual calendar to remind and inspire you to act accordingly.

Every anniversary requires flowers, no exceptions, either delivered by you or delivered by the florist from you. She gets to say to her co-workers that the flowers are for her anniversary. A few weeks or months later, send more flowers. Then she gets to say they are for her *other* anniversary. It may be possible she is the only person at work receiving flowers due to a multiplicity of anniversaries. Her co-workers will demand explanations, and each time she gets to tell them that you never forget any anniversary, that she still receives flowers for the day you started dating. If your friends call to complain, tell them to read this book and that you treat your wife with the respect she deserves. *Get over it!*

(By the way, I am still working on all this myself. I believe my wife will say, if asked about me, "He does better than most.")

Reminisce with her about some special thing, dinner, place or event you both enjoyed on a specific anniversary. Talk to her about it, discuss it with her, and you can relive wonderful experiences again and again.

For each successive anniversary, strive to do something unique. Let's say it's the anniversary of the day you first met. Do something that day different than the normal daily routine, making new memories for this occasion. Do this for every anniversary. It does not have to be a grand and royal affair. Just talk to her and love her. After all, why would you not want to have the same feelings you had at that special moment together at the same time you're making precious new moments?

Wedding anniversaries should be celebrated by just the two of you. You may have additional celebrations with family or friends also but plan one with just her. *Remember, she is the love of your life.* If you have kids, they should be included at some point as they should see the joy and love you have for each other. Celebrating with friends depends on how close you are with those friends and if you feel comfortable celebrating with them. They may have been at your wedding, but often friends feel celebrating your wedding anniversary is imposing on your private life. You will know if it is appropriate to ask friends. *Just be sure you first ask your wife after she knows you have planned a celebration for your anniversary.*

However, decide to celebrate and do something for just the two of you. Find someplace to be alone, talk to each other, hold each other, and take this time to reaffirm your love for her as if it was the first time.

Should you tell her you love her on every anniversary, whether it is your wedding anniversary or one of those "other" anniversaries? Absolutely! But, if you have been reading this book and absorbing some of its contents, you already tell her every day that you love her. On anniversaries, however, tell her in special ways and several times. Will she grow tired of hearing it? *Never!*

I like to plan each anniversary on its own merit by how it represents different events in our lives and may require different celebrations. For example, for the first time we met, I would try to recreate in context the place and time of day. The reason I said "in context" is because I may want to celebrate this anniversary in another location. I want to bring back that moment in time so we can relive it again together. For, the first date, of course recreate place and time, something about what you discussed, maybe ask her on a date for that night, and treat the evening like it was your first date. Like in the movies, you get to go home with the girl, *unless you really mess things up.*

As for the day you actually proposed, try it again! *Go ahead. You know what the answer will be* (you hope). For this occasion, consider celebrating in a totally different place than the first time. Why? *I will never tire of proposing to the love of my life.* The possibilities for what comes next are endless.

The wedding anniversary we talked about can be celebrated with or without company. If "with company" is appropriate, celebrate it with as many as you feel comfortable. However, never lose touch with the fact that, when you both decided on the specific time and date you were to be married, it was for many reasons. Hopefully, and most importantly, you felt it was your day and no one else's.

No matter if thousands of other couples were getting married on the same day, this day, *this* time belonged to you. Plan a celebration some place for a party of two and only two, a place to cherish your love, a place to share your soul, a place to remember why together you chose that day as "your day" and the reasons you asked for her hand in the first place.

Why is there more than one anniversary? Because you can never show your love for her and what she means to you only once per year.

Chapter 28

Surprise! Surprise!
(There should be more than one surprise per year, too!)

Just like it reads—surprise, surprise. Do you surprise her once a day, a week, a month? There should be more than one day per year when you know *she deserves the best.....*

You know your companion better than anyone else, or you should, so you will know if she likes surprises. There has probably been a study done that tells us how little men know about their wives. There is a simple way to find out if she likes surprises: ask her, *"Do you like surprises?"* She will answer and my internal study *(It's my internal study, because then I don't have to publish the results)* says the answer will be: *"Yes, I do like surprises."* Does she like surprises that embarrass her? Well, of course not. Would you? No one likes being embarrassed even if only in front of family.

Maybe her answer will be, *"No, I don't like surprises."* It's time for that communication we discussed to kick in here. Find out why. Be supportive, be gentle and be caring with your discussion. Ask and then *listen*. She may not like surprises because she fears you will embarrass her. She knows you better than you will ever know yourself.

Surprise is spontaneous, fun, and exciting. Surprise shows you are thinking of her. How often do you plan surprises? If the notion strikes, then you strike, with all the pomp and circumstance you can muster.

What kinds of surprises can you plan? To name a few: show up at her work with flowers, bring her flowers at home in the middle of the day, call her after you get to work and tell her you are taking her out for dinner tonight, buy a gift and give it to her during dinner, buy a gift and leave it on her pillow before bed, rub her feet, massage her shoulders, make dinner, tell her mid-week the two you are going on a romantic weekend on Friday (*or Thursday*), call her when you get to work and plan a lunch date, pick her up for lunch and hand her a rose, tell her she looks beautiful and you both should forget work and spend a romantic afternoon together, find that catalog she was looking at a few days ago and order that nice dress she so subtly pointed out to you, wash her car, call her and say *I love you*, pick her up from work with a gift or flowers, or pick her up from work with a gift *and* flowers, tell her in the morning to pick out a nice dress because you have a surprise for her after work, bring a small gift home every day after work for a week, after she leaves for work one day stay home and do that "thing" she has been wanting you to do for weeks or months, declare that today is her "virtual birthday" or when you get home in the evening tell her to forget dinner because you have reservations for dinner at a very posh restaurant, etc.

You don't need to be a professional creative consultant to dream up some nice, loving, caring surprises. Surprises can be miniscule, large, or anywhere in between. Larger, more complex surprises may take planning for flawless execution. If you plan a nice surprise of a long weekend, she will enjoy a little advance notice to have time to prepare. *No,* you have not lost your element of surprise! You accomplished that with: *"Hey, let's get out of town this weekend."*

Now that you have told her about the weekend getaway, you both have time to plan a really good time. As opposed to Friday afternoon at 5:00 saying, *"Let's go out of town this weekend.* Nothing is packed, she doesn't know where you intend to go, and all you have accomplished is creating a lot of stress. You have managed a surprise all right, *but a not so happy surprise.*

Totally spontaneous surprises don't always create stress, embarrassment or bad feelings. They should create fun and excitement. Keep those words *fun* and *excitement* in mind and you can't go wrong. Be aware of what you are expecting her to do and realize she may need some time to prepare.

Probably the best surprise is a simple one like getting home early and having dinner prepared when she gets home, along with flowers and a gift. It goes like this, if she calls on the way home and wants to know when you're getting home or what you want for dinner, say, *"I thought about steak, baked potato, salad, green beans, dinner rolls and apple crisp for dessert."* When you hear that long sigh that says, *"It's been a long day, I'm tired and I'm not going to prepare all of that tonight."* Before she says anything, you tell her you have all of that prepared and it is waiting for her when she gets home. You can both sit down and enjoy dinner. Afterwards, you'll clean up while she finds a place to relax. She will appreciate this simple yet nice surprise. Maybe you can give her a soothing foot rub and you both can retire early and enjoy an evening without the television.

Large surprises, as I said, take careful planning so that they do not overwhelm you or her. Usually birthday parties and such tend to be larger and don't require a vast amount of time and effort, and they don't usually fall into the *stressful* category. The more people who know about the surprise, the more likely it is it won't be much of a surprise anyway. When a surprise reaches epic proportions, it tends not to convey your true intention behind the surprise. All you are wanting to say is, *"I love you very much, and I want to show you I love you every day."* So, don't go too overboard on the surprises.

I find numerous small surprises are the best and most rewarding for both of you. Like her hearing the words *I love you,* she won't ever get tired of all those little surprises because she never knows when to expect the next *surprise!*

Chapter 29

Mother's Day

(Near the end for a reason, and if you don't know why by now, you really do need help.)

Wow!

Mother—the person from whom you learned the meaning of love, feeling, and caring. Everyone reminds us to call our Mother on Mother's Day. If you don't see your Mother every day, then you should be calling her more often than just on Mother's Day. So, if you have not talked to your Mom today, *"Call your MOM!!!!"* Do it right now; don't wait. This book is not going anywhere, so call her.

Ring...ring...ring....ring.... *"Hi, Mom!!!!!"* See how simple that was?

Have you ever stopped to think about what your Mother has done for you? She taught you love, feeling, caring, sorrow, how to clean your room *(maybe you didn't do it, but she did teach you how),* how to dress yourself, how to feed yourself, how to talk, how to stand, how to walk, how to cook, and the list goes on and on.

Why did your Mom do all this? Because your Mother never stops loving you or teaching you. Why? Because she is a woman. Would she have done all that and more if she had a choice? *Yes,* over and over again. Just as mothers have been doing since the beginning of God's creation.

This is not to say your Father does not love you He loves you just as much and for most of us he was involved with the things we just discussed. Fathers often teach you other things like taking out the trash, mowing the lawn, driving the car, changing a tire, and how to stay out of Mom's way when she's not feeling well. But you refine your knowledge and skills taught by your Father based on what your Mother teaches you. Think back. Dad told you to do something in a certain way. What did you most likely do later? You asked Mom how to do it, because you needed that reassurance you were doing it correctly. Mom is always there, always teaching, always refining, and always loving.

Moms have usually put in longer work days than Dads since the day they were first married. And when that first bundle of joy came along, yep, Mom's workday just got longer, usually because many fathers didn't help when they should.

The average mother manages more uncooperative *staff*, more crises, more projects, more business decisions, more personal decisions, more family decisions, more logistical decisions, more transportation decisions, and more financial decisions than any corporate CEO in the world. She does these things daily, without fail, without complaining, and many, many times she does them by herself without help from anyone. In addition, she is your personal nurse when you are ill, your personal launderer, your personal maid, your personal chef, and she insures you look your best before you leave the house. Can you say, *"Thanks, Mom!!!!!"*?

"What is the most important thing your Mother taught you as you were growing up?" Hint: Go way back to the Dedication, close to the front, there it is...... If you find yourself reading this book in the company of a woman or there happens to be a woman close by, ask her. No doubt her answer will be: *"How to treat women!"* Your Mom taught you this every day of your life. You may not have been *listening,* but she taught you.

She taught you how to act anytime you found yourself around any female: your sister, your neighborhood friends, your classmates, your cousins, your Grandmother, your Mother's friends. Think back, you will remember she taught you how to treat your companion on that very first date. Most likely just about every other date afterwards she would say something like, *"Mind your manners, now."*

If you don't believe Mother's teach you every important aspect of life you need to know, then why is it that *Mother Nature does everything and Father Time does only one thing?*

Chapter 30

Father's Day

(Relax, enjoy, it's a day for you to realize what life has given you.)

Dad's day—if you are a Dad, you already know the joys of fatherhood. Forsaking any medical reasons, any man can be a father but not every man can be a Dad, Daddy or Pop. I will add that some "fathers" can be real Dads, too. Dad takes you places, plays games with you, let's you do things *Mom won't let you do,* and teaches you those outside things we talked about earlier. Some fathers, most unlike Dads, do whatever it is father's do, which usually translates into *not much*, and they have very little involvement in their kids' lives. Thank God for Mommy's and Daddy's. My Dad was busy like all Dads, but he was always there, always helping, always ready to *straighten* me out when the occasion called for it. I was like most kids growing up. I knew both of my parents were dumb and didn't know much about anything past helping with my school work on occasion, or *so I thought.*

It was not until I was around 35 that I magically realized my parents were not that dumb and, to my surprise, they were actually quite knowledgeable! It seemed all at once memories flooded in of *I remember that, Mom did this, Dad did that*, and so on.

Real Dads teach both sons and daughters about life. Not all real Dads teach their sons and daughters about things to do with the house, the car, etc. Sadly, some only teach their sons, many won't teach their daughters.

Something happened here, and something happened there, and suddenly I came to a stark realization Mom and Dad knew all about this stuff. Yes, they had tried over the years in many ways to let me know what to do, or at least let me know how to handle certain "situations" as they arose, hoping I had matured to a point where I would listen. *Did I mention I was a slow learner?*

Dad's Day

Dad should have some latitude on his day. He should get a nice gift, get to watch his favorite television event, have his favorite lunch or dinner, be kind of lazy for the day *(like this day is any different than any other day, as Mom might say).*

If you are a Dad, what do you want to do on Father's Day? Hopefully, you would want to be with your kids and your wife, because you have the whole day to do anything you want, the whole day to spend with the ones you love.

There is a reason Mother's Day and Father's Day are on Sunday. Don't lose sight of this reason. Real

Dad's spend time with their families, real Dad's teach their children how to love and what love means. And Sundays are days for family time.

If you need help here, you can always ask your Mom. She will know, or your wife will. You may also get a step-by-step outline in 1st Corinthians, Chapter 13, Verses 4-7 (NIV). In case you don't have a reference handy, here's what it says:

> 4 *Love is patient, love is kind. It does not envy, it does not boast, it is not proud.* 5 *It does not dishonor others, it is not self-seeking, it is not easily angered, it keeps no record of wrongs.* 6 *Love does not delight in evil but rejoices with the truth.* 7 *It always protects, always trusts, always hopes, always perseveres.*

Not a believer? No problem. These words are about loving your fellow human being. If you don't love, you can't be loved.

You wouldn't be a real Dad or a real Father without a significant amount of help. Think back through the years and remember the times the love of your life did something for you. She said, *"That's ok. I'll do it."* Remember all those times she was sure to remind you not to forget a special date, a birthday, an anniversary, Mother's Day, or even that big meeting at work. Think how she lets you know when you needed to change shirts, or wear different trousers, or said, "Those shoes don't match." *(My personal favorite. I only have two pair of shoes.)*

Now it's time to let her know how much you appreciate her love, her dedication, her perseverance. Surprise her with a gift. Tell her you know its Father's Day, but you wanted to let her know what she means to you. Send flowers to her at work and put on the card: *I love you.* She will tell her friends: *"See, I even get flowers from my husband on Father's Day!"*

If you don't have kids, then make sure you visit or at least talk to your Dad on Father's Day. If you visit, do something with your Dad, but don't forget Mom either.

If you're doing something only for you and your Dad, fine, but when you finish, get Mom and take her out so all of you can celebrate.

Dads, Mom's, wives, and significant others are always there for you, whenever and wherever you may be. In our world today, you can call them any time any place. So, *call them,* see them as often as you can, make the time to interact with them, for all too soon they won't be on the other end of that phone anymore. Yet they will be in your thoughts to remind you what is right, what is wrong, and to love you.

Cherish your gift of life, cherish your kids, cherish your life's companion. Tell them today you love them, tell them every day you love them, *tell them......life changes when you least expect it.*

Mikal Haney

Since the beginning of time women have endured.

Chapter 31

The Workplace

(One day it will occur. I hope I get to see that day when there is equality for women in the workplace.)

What is work? A very large or very small place known to most of us simply as *work*. We say *I'm going to work*, or *this guy at work*, or *I hate work* or *at work we do this*. Here is a definition of the term *workplace* from a free online dictionary:

Work-place
Noun

1. A place, such as an office or factory, where people are employed.
2. The work setting in general: *"one of the last male bastions of the American workplace"*

Does this reek of male chauvinism, the Stone Age, or what? Maybe it is a good definition of about every workplace in America. Unfortunately, this sentiment and practice is echoed around the world in one fashion or another, but I'm going to stick with the United States of America. I have experience in the American workplace and my brief observations outside of the U.S.A. could have been tainted by my surroundings, my perception, maybe my misunderstanding of the situation. I'm going out on a limb here to say that I suspect this type of reprehensible attitude is commonplace the world over. If indeed it turns out I am wrong, please accept my humble and heartfelt apology. I will be the first person to tell you I have little multinational knowledge. I am sure, however, about one thing: male bastions do flourish in the United States of America. I see it every day everywhere and not only in the workplace.

Women have been operating successful "corporations" before man even defined the word. For years, women have been managing the home with little or no assistance from their spouses. *Thank God for Moms!* They helped when and where possible.

Many men, whether they are blue collar or at the top of the white-collar ladder, have no earthly idea what is required to manage a household, especially a household with kids. In case you have forgotten or chose to skip ahead, we lightly touched on Mom's accomplishments back in the Chapter on Mother's Day, though I remind you, we only *touched* on the countless efforts and the workload of Moms everywhere.

In today's world, Moms not only run the household corporation, many of them work full time as well. Try giving that task to your husband or that Manager, Director, or President down the corridor who likes to boast how he is *together* and on top of everything all the time. The results in most instances would be failure.

It goes something like this for those stay-at-home Moms: *The washer is leaking, the kids are fighting in the next room, one of them is crying, the TV is blaring away with no one watching, there's Jell-O in the dryer, the clothes hamper is a fort, the laundry basket with the last two loads of clean clothes is outside full of kittens, pick up the kids at school, go to the cleaners, go grocery shopping for dinner tonight. Her husband is bringing home some colleagues from work and the hot tub repairman is there. Why is the hot tub repairman there? Because the hot tub has to be fixed so her husband can relax after a hard day at the office!* **Yeah, RIGHT!!!!!!!!!!**

Add on all that to a Mom that works full time. While nothing at home changes, the working Mom has to manage all those *little* chores remotely and do her full-time job at the same time (which often includes doing her boss's job, too, WITH MUCH LESS PAY). Oh, by the way—those male bastions don't believe that the working woman ever experiences a *hard day at the office.* The working woman is expected to arrive home before her husband, clean everything up, prepare a veritable feast, settle the kids, freshen up so she looks like a super model on the cover of Vogue, and be at her husband's beck and call. Then she cleans up everything after dinner, insures the kids don't disturb his quite time, then prepares him for the next day. When she has completed this, then she does for him whatever else he dreams up since, of course, he did have a *hard day*.

Are there working Moms and Dads that share these responsibilities? Sure, there are, usually because the Mom forces the issue and makes it happen. Was this the case only a few years ago? No? Only in the past few decades (a very few decades) has this "sharing" concept come along. If you take your own poll, and everyone is truthful, I think you will find that male dominance is still very prominent in our society. It is changing as we speak (very slowly); however, progress is excruciatingly painful and changing only because women are making the change happen.

Why is this scenario played out over and over again each day? I don't know, but to find the answer, we should probably ask a woman. Most of the things we have talked about involve kids and their Moms who would do things for them at any cost (as would many Dads as well).

Often women find themselves as personal servants to their boyfriends, too; it's not only a married thing. We will discuss the manager-to-employee scenario a little later. No one stands up and says I want a lifetime of personal servitude. Sometimes a woman does it for fear of reprisal if she does not perform the duties a man feels she should. If you ask the husband or boyfriend, you will likely hear: *"That is what she is supposed to do."* Really?

Thankfully, sometime in the 20th century, women learning from their fore-sisters began to make changes and started chipping away at those many decades (several hundred years) of male domination. My observations tell me women are making headway. I'm not sure how much longer it will take until it is truly eradicated. I do see progress—just not enough. Will there ever be total equality? No, simply because men will continue to dominate at every opportunity, bringing to bear their ancestral moronic roots. That is, until they are injured, or their fragile egos are threatened, then you can be assured they will go running to a woman. Maybe that is because of some animalistic trait that causes them to hasten back to where they feel superior. Maybe they are simply mentally unable to accept that, in many ways, they are the weak ones and women only allow them to feel superior. *Remember, "One does mean one."*

Ok, I am ready. Let's hear it. *"Can a woman bench press 200 pounds?"* is one the first idiotic comments made by most men. The answer, *"No, some cannot." If they could, you would not hear them bragging about it either. Most of the men making a statement like that cannot do it either."* Then we hear a lengthy diatribe about how women are weak and frail, and some men even say stupid (*now that's an unintelligent comment*). Trust me, you do not want to be on the opposing side of a woman when you have just called her stupid. A more intelligent question coming from the bastions of American men should be, "Do women want perfect equality with men?" My guess is that women like to be treated with respect and dignity, and women want to be paid equally for the job they do if it's the same job done by a male counterpart. Then it should be equal pay to the penny. Women want to be doted on. Get a clue! They dote on you every day of your miserable, *"I'm stronger, better and smarter than you"* life. One final comment on throwing around that phrase *weaker sex:* don't push your luck, women possess knowledge men will never have and they are blessed with the ability to use it.

Real men, real Dads, like to take care of women. They like being nice to women, and they understand women should be treated with respect, respect in every way. If you are nice to someone, then most likely that someone will be nice to you.

Now, where do the not-so-subtle but brutal inequalities lay? **The Workplace**. Why? Regardless of what a man might say about what happens in his home regarding his kingdom, be certain of one thing, only a very small part of his boasting bears any resemblance to fact. Therefore, his ego and thirst for superiority must manifest somewhere.

In the workplace, office, or anywhere men and women work together, women's salaries are the most contemptuous blatant example of men abusing their power, totally unequaled by any other act except for the ones that are criminal in nature. Probably the top three areas women point to as inequality in the workplace are: (1) salary, (2) sexual harassment, and

(3) often being ignored or even ridiculed. At every level where women work *(I know, except for the military)*, their salaries are much below their male counterparts. In some cases, their salaries are based on the mentality of *"Your husband works, so you don't need a lot of money."* **The words that come to my mind are not for print.**

I believe the explanation for this anomaly is that 80% *(my internal survey again)*, maybe even more than 80%, of men believe women are inferior to men. If my internal survey is wrong, I will graciously accept correction and publish my error, *as long as the correction comes from a woman.* Men have paid women less money for an equivalent position. Every woman I know having the power to set men's salaries will pay the industry norms or above, based on skill level.

Women work harder and smarter, and they produce more than their male counterparts. You won't find many surveys, if any, that depict performance numbers when both men and women are involved in the same role, especially a report reflecting individual performance. Women find themselves with larger workloads and a greater number of employees to manage as compared to their male counterparts. Problem employees are oftentimes moved to the women's work unit. Even with all these *extra duties,* women usually complete their tasks ahead of the men. Still, women are frequently passed over for salary increases and promotions. Men cite the reason for their decisions as *"Men are the bread winners. They have families to feed,"* even if the male manager knows the woman is a single mother or, for that matter, just single. To this day, single men still enjoy much higher salaries than single women.

Women are better managers than men because they see the whole picture—the person the personality, work ethics—and they *listen*. (*Remember, we talked about communication when only one side communicates.*) Here's an example of how many men communicate:

"You listen. I'll talk."
or
"You are supposed to know what I want."
or
"You should be writing this down."

Now there are some classics! Ask a working woman how many times she has heard those phrases.

Communication, by my definition, is both the manager and the employee talking, both listening, and then both discussing what each other has to say. Yes, I know the ultimate decision and responsibility lie with the manager (man or woman). *Good* managers will tell you they listen to their employees when making important decisions, while being fair and objective toward the individuals and the decision at hand.

More often than not, the male manager does not listen and usually blames an employee when he makes a bad decision.

Some companies are working toward equalizing the salary situation. Please read that sentence one more time and note the words *working toward equalizing*. I daresay it will be sometime before women's salaries come close to being equal.

Let's discuss other areas where women find themselves short in the *"Hey, I'm a person too, you know"* category of the American worker. Making coffee, fetching coffee, cleaning up the lunch room, stocking the lunch room refrigerator *(usually out of her own pocket)*, having to laugh at the manager's stupid if not sexist jokes, being subjected to sexual harassment by male peers on a daily basis, having a parking space that is the farthest one from the building, being required to wear high fashion clothing *(to look nice for male employees)*, being ignored in meetings, being expected to take the meeting minutes, scheduling company parties, planning the company parties, working the company parties, cleaning up after the company parties, running errands for the boss, running errands for the boss's family, often being the first person to arrive at work and the last person to leave work, being chastised when asking for vacation time *(Who is going to do the work when you're away?)*, and on and on, just to scratch the surface.

I have even witnessed male managers taking their

female counterparts to lunch with them for the purpose of impressing a client. They take a female employee, knowing the person wouldn't dream of causing a stir for fear of losing her job, or the woman is lied to and doesn't realize until the arrival that she is not part of the conversation. When women are introduced, the man glazes over her title, making her sound paltry or insignificant, while quickly moving onto the business at hand, which if we knew the truth the *business at hand* was probably researched, designed, and created by a woman. Ok, now you are saying, *"HEY! Men can research, design, and create, too."* Yes, you are correct; however, not one single man has ever researched, designed, and created anything without the assistance of a woman. Once more with emphasis, **not one single man has ever researched, designed and created anything without the assistance of a woman.** *Yeah, sure. I know he was born by a woman.* I mean when he presents his great idea, plan, new concept or whatever, he had plenty, and I mean plenty, of help from a woman, or multiple women, during the process.

Where does this all end? If I knew the answer to that question, then I would be called a soothsayer, which I am not. I at least know one thing for sure: Moms didn't train their little boys this way. It is a learned behavior they garnered along the way or one taught by their "fathers". I sincerely believe greed is a huge factor—greed for power, money, or an insatiable need to control other human beings to make it known they have the power.

I believe the end of all this male workplace dominance begins with more women in decision-making roles. I have had the pleasure of working for women in various roles during my life. I have lived quite a few years, and I can say, *"I have never been treated unfairly by any female manager."* Have I been treated unfairly by male managers? Absolutely! But, being a man, I was not treated as unfairly as my female counterparts. A sign that things are beginning to change is that more women than men are graduating from our colleges and universities. We have women mayors, governors, senators and representatives. However, change is coming too slowly, in my opinion.

Why not a woman president? With a woman president, I foresee fewer wars, better businesses, more emphasis on food for our homeless, better care and education for our children, better health benefits, less unemployment, and stronger ties with some of our world neighbors.

Why not a woman president? *I, for one, hope I get to see that day! I know whom I will be voting for!*

Chapter 32

Afterthoughts

(Accomplishment, Reason, Reward, etc.)

Oh, where to begin? Let's stay with that workplace thing a little longer. Ladies, the next time you do some grilling in the backyard, set up a video camera and watch how many times the Grill Master yells for you to get something for him. Also remind him who prepared the rest of *his* great meal. Another thing, if you don't believe this is a male-dominated world, then why do some famous female writers often use their initials instead of using their first names?

Communication

Communication is the ultimate foundation of any relationship, whether it is a work, personal or romantic relationship. You must have two-way conversations with your spouse, co-worker, manager or significant other. On a personal level, if you fail to maintain anything but full communication between the two of you, you lose much of the joy in your relationship. You may be upset about something she purchased that day or any number of other things you can find to be upset about. You may believe she does not realize you are upset. Don't count on the premise "she does not realize" as she is more intelligent than you give her credit for. She is most likely very aware of your feelings and is waiting to see what your reaction is going to be. If you don't talk to her about it, you may never know why she did the thing she did. Some men say they can't talk to women because women won't listen. Unless you are being a complete idiot, she will always listen. If she is upset and not speaking, then ask her why.

If she doesn't want to talk about it, persist. If she still refuses to discuss it with you, then at the very least say to her, *"I understand you may need some alone time to think and I respect that. When you are ready to talk I will be here to **listen**."*

I have already mentioned the concept that every time she talks about a problem or concern, she does not necessarily want you to "fix" it. Almost always, she simply wants you to listen. She will tell you if she needs help to sort it out, but to know what she wants, you must be *listening*!

What do you talk about? Anything! Just engaging in conversation with her and sharing information with her allows both of you to better understand each other. Besides, a pleasing benefit from all this talking is that you get to spend hours looking into her eyes and maybe even holding her hand.

Let's think of a few places to have these conversations: while walking in a park, while seated under a shade tree, when shopping, over a long relaxing dinner, or while walking on the beach, sitting in the car, at home, in the yard or on a Ferris wheel. Get the picture? Anywhere.

You didn't learn to talk without first listening. Communication begins with listening. If you initiate a conversation with anyone, you first expect them to hear you and listen to what you have to say. They expect you to hear them and listen to what they have to say as well. *Remember to think before you speak.*

Most importantly, *listen*. You may find "that thing she did today" was for you, but you were too busy *running your mouth* to hear what she said.

Should you keep secrets from your spouse or girlfriend? There are several opinions on this subject. My point of view says yes and no. Yes, concerning gift giving and surprises. No, when you expect to have a meaningful relationship. Does this mean that you should say, "*I think that outfit makes you look less than pleasing to the eye*"? Yes, if you have good communication with her as she will appreciate your candor. She may not like it, but she will understand you are sincere. That overused cliché "*Does this make me look bad?*" is just that—overused. Not many women will say that to their husbands. Are there some gross and inconsiderate men that will say that to their wives? Absolutely. Even without the question being asked. I bring to bear the importance of communications and point out once again: when you hear a woman say. *"men are pigs,"* there is only one sex to blame.

The area of sharing information and keeping

secrets is touchy and you must handle each situation on its own merit. My personal rule of thumb goes like this: if it feels wrong, don't do it. Being truthful with anyone is the right thing to do. Bad results from secrets in a relationship, romantic or not, can escalate quickly and could have been prevented if honest conversation had taken place.

Shopping

She is going to go shopping and you have to shop yourself on occasion, at least when those important dates I mentioned roll around. There will be days when she wants to shop alone or with her friends. On those other days, don't be afraid to ask her if you can go along. I know you may hate shopping. *Get over it!*

It is no big deal. It beats sitting around the house watching the tube or dreaming about that pet project you said you were going to start months ago. When you go shopping with her, you get to see what interests her, which goes a long way when searching for that perfect gift. You can ask her about certain articles of clothing or jewelry as to her specific taste. You get to spend time with her in a relaxed setting. She can ask if you like a certain look or style of clothing. You can tell her what types of clothing you like to wear.

The possibilities are endless and you would not even have had a clue if you hadn't gone shopping with her. You can still lie to your friends and tell them she dragged you shopping, yet she will be sure to brag to her friends how very nice it was for you accompany her shopping.

What Women Do for Men

Women go to great lengths to please men. It doesn't even have to be their husbands. They will do it for their boyfriend, bosses or fathers. A woman will work all day then come home to begin her second job: taking care of you. Yes, I know there are husbands who take care of themselves, but we are talking about the majority, not the few.

All the while you may be sitting there doing nothing and most likely complaining about something at home or work. Yet, she turns right around and does it all over again the next day and every day thereafter.

You can see other examples of this play out in your daily life if you are observant. *(I know it may be hard for you to concentrate long enough to observe anything, but try.)* At work, you may hear a female co-worker talking about something she did earlier for her husband or boss because she knows he likes it, or you overhear your wife telling a friend, *"Oh, I fold his socks together so he does not have to look for the pairs."* (Really? You can't tell the difference between brown and black?). If, you don't believe these examples, ask any woman how often she does things simply to please a man. Her answer? *Many, many times!!!*

Women exert a lot of time and energy insuring the fragile egos of men remain unscathed. Few men will go to any extreme for a woman.

Control - Who Makes the Rules?

In many cases, people get married, then suddenly the man is the boss and ruler of all things. *"You will do what I say, when I say!"* he says.

Lots of men believe they must be *in control* because they are the *man of the house* and will make all the decisions. The thought is: *"Man is King, woman is servant."* Talk about the lack of progress! Men haven't progressed much since those *good ole'* medieval days. Men definitely can't echo this phrase said about women: *"You've come a long way, baby."*

Control is one of those things that drive some men to seek control beyond sanity. Some types of personalities seem to crave, and even demand, to be in control. Maybe it is a defense mechanism keeping them from becoming embarrassed in front of other people. Maybe they are selfish, scared little boys. Maybe these men have been conditioned to believe they must control the situation, whether at home or work. If we knew the truth, however, they are probably more successful at work than at home. When a man tells you, "What I say goes," that may not always turn out to be the case. Some men like to tell everyone they are the ultimate ruler of their castle. *(There is part of the problem. To women it is a home.)* I have seen just the opposite on several occasions. Women have uncanny ways to express their perspectives and cast their votes when a situation warrants it, and usually it only takes one vote (hers).

Generally, rules in the workplace are made by men or a small group of men. These rules usually don't take into account women in the workplace. Women are thought of afterwards or you will hear, "Oh, yeah, we have to do that, too."

An example in an office I observed, all the conference table tops were clear glass. A decision made by men not thinking of the ramifications—or maybe they did, which is normal for many men in the workplace.

Don't understand this example? Ask a woman.

To sum up this control thing, it can be defined as *abuse of power*, plain and simple.

Men Are Clueless!

Simply put and very true. I've watched men's expression's in crowded restaurants when their wives sit there quietly as their husbands' ogle another woman. When one of these men's loving wife finally says something out of sheer embarrassment, he stares blankly at her and invariably takes one more look before returning his eyes back to his own table. Wives certainly do endure humiliation for their husbands' behavior. You could ask the husband a hundred questions concerning his behavior, and he would never ever grasp the obvious.

And what about wedding rings? I'd like to see a survey about what percentage of married men wear a wedding ring. You hear these words, "I can't wear one because it is too dangerous in my job" or "I don't wear jewelry." Maybe you can sell the first excuse if your job is in a factory and you are surrounded by complex machinery, but you can certainly wear it when you are not at work. The second excuse falls into the category of "You can't sell that ice to an Eskimo." My guess is your wife is expected to wear her wedding ring all the time.

Let me offer a couple of reasons I have heard women give about her husband not wearing a wedding ring: *He doesn't want anyone to know he's married. If he doesn't wear a wedding ring, he might get "lucky" or if he doesn't wear a wedding ring, he can hit on women.* I have had men tell me these same reasons also.

I believe that, if you love your wife, you will wear a ring. If you think women you are hitting on believe you're not married, that laughter you hear behind your back is those women laughing at your stupidity. Would you like to know just how stupid?

You can't hide it. If you are married and not wearing a ring, most single and all married women will still know you are married. *Clue: they can see it in your eyes. Now, do you see why those women are laughing?*

Here are some simple questions to check for

yourself whether men are clueless. Ask any man these questions: What is your wife wearing today? What color are your wife's eyes? Is she wearing a suit, a dress or pantsuit? Does she have on a necklace? Does she have on earrings? Is she wearing makeup? Do the kids have any appointments today?

From the answers to these questions, you can easily see: *"Men are clueless."*

Ever heard these? *This is too hard for a woman,* or *Women can't do this.*

Many men have been openly and justifiably humiliated by uttering these very stupid statements. You say, *"Well, a woman can't pick up a tractor tire like those strong men on television."* No, and most likely neither can you! Be patient. You will have your turn in the proverbial barrel if you utter one of those condescending phrases once too often.

Women are not like men. Thank God for this. Unlike men, women will not take this hubris as a challenge. Most women scoff when they hear these words. Before you decide to engage in a one on one with a woman, you might want to check your ego at the door.

Ego

That conscious psyche we all possess as men and women, although men's egos often fail to fit within the confines of their brain cavity. A great number of men's egos fail to be limited by space, that space which we have yet to define, that space characterized as being outside our own galaxy. This egotistical phenomenon is but one reason for the existence of fear and need for control, and it is the biggest reason men treat women as inferior and strive to limit women's professional and personal lives.

Yes, there are women with exceptional egos. If one were to keep a tally, say in your office building, I am guessing you would need more paper for the men's column before you even surveyed one floor.

You can witness a good example of "ego creep" for yourself even with no women present. The next time you are with a group of men, mention some fictitious fantasy involving a display of unusual strength, prowess, great accomplishment or, lest we forget, superior sexuality. Sit back and wait for the myriad of stories that are told, each one more adventurous than the last.

Place a woman in this assemblage when the men are comfortable with her presence and the stories become even more outrageous—to impress her, no doubt. Is ego the only driving force behind men's "normal" behavior? No. Enter masculinity and virility; now the egos go off the charts.

Masculinity and Virility

Women are attracted to masculinity and virility. You may ask, "Are these the only traits women look for in men?" Ask a man and most often the answer will be, "Well, yeah."

Ask that same man what other traits women look for and the list will include numerous variations of masculinity and virility and usually nothing more. Maybe money will be thrown in somewhere because many men believe all women want is "the raging hulk", a superior body, and money. Truthfully, men spend as much or more money than women. Let's go back to that office building tally sheet, this time surveying who spends the most money. Men will lose this one nearly every time. I am not talking about the support for a family. They buy *toys*, lots of *toys*! The purchases are usually disguised as technology, and women hear the words, "I need this for my job."

What men do not realize is, while women may be first attracted by masculinity and virility, their final assessment rests with numerous other factors. If you are interested in what other factors women use to assess men, read Chapters 1 through 31.

Women will never yield to or accept physical attraction only.

Walk the Talk

If you speak it, then do it. If you speak it and don't do it, prepare for a melancholy lonely existence with *no* long-term relationships in your future. In this context, I define "long term" as that time shortly after you open your mouth and possibly another few minutes. If this kind of life is for you, fine. I hope you are never in a position to need or want another person's assistance. Only fools believe they can travel through life without the relationship of another human being.

How many times have you said or heard, *"You can't believe everything he says"?* It only takes a few conversations with people to establish you as less than believable. Not one male or female will ever become a trusted friend or companion to a non-truthful storyteller.

Hypocrisy is learned; you learn from other hypocrites. Often it is merely the easy way out. After a short time, you even begin to believe your own stories, even when everyone around you knows your words are only half truths.

The real trouble comes when you must remember all of your yarns, then the world turns from inviting to menacing. There is only one way out when you realize your façade is crumbling. Truth and apology! If you are not true to yourself, you cannot be true to others.

There is *a road less traveled,* a road many men have never seen and some unfortunately will never see. That road being the *narrow road,* the one traveled by brave, compassionate, strong men that understand women are the most important part of their lives and valued equal companions.

You may have heard these words in the past:

"Wives, submit yourselves to your own husbands as you do to the Lord. For the husband is

the head of the wife as Christ is the head of the church, his body, of which he is the Savior. Now as the church submits to Christ, so also wives should submit to their husbands in everything."

Many men will be very up front in uttering the above words. The part many won't tell you is the passage preceding the one above:

"Submit to one another out of reverence for Christ."

Here are words these selfish men don't want to hear:

"In this same way, husbands ought to love their wives as their own bodies. He who loves his wife loves himself. After all, no one ever hated their own body, but they feed and care for their body, just as Christ does the church—for we are members of his body. For this reason, a man will leave his father and mother and be united to his wife, and the two will become one flesh."

Not a believer? No problem. Still there is not one single man who ever accomplished one single thing without the assistance of a woman.

"One really means one." Neither you nor any other man will succeed in life without the assistance of a woman, whether she is your mother, your wife, your co-worker, your boss, your friend, your sister, your neighbor, or maybe a complete stranger. At some point in your adult life, a woman will be there for you as you should be there for her as well.

Respect and Forgiveness

You cannot be respected unless first you respect. You hear people say respect is earned. I lean toward showing people respect first, and then I receive their respect. Just as you can never be forgiven unless first you forgive. if you get in a spat with your wife, be the one to apologize first. There is no "I" in "One."

Why Do I Believe Women Should Have More Power?

Commitment

Daily, I witness women with much greater commitment to every aspect of life than men. They have commitment to children even if they are not mothers. They have a deeper commitment to work ethics. Women have nearly always done more with less than most men. Not just with less money either. They usually end up at the bottom of the list for supplies and tools to perform their daily work tasks. Remember *who is making the rules?* Women have a commitment to family, friends and co-workers. And, most importantly, women's commitment to life is immeasurable compared to men.

Immeasurable is the number of times in any given day where a man asks a woman for help. These men that are asking women for help an immeasurable number of times each day do it without *thinking,* and they do not realize their woeful inadequacies. (Now, there's a thought, *men thinking.)* Women are solving men's problems every day so they will look good to the boss, while those same men are telling the boss they arrived at the solution themselves. To carry this a bit further, it wouldn't make any difference if a man told the boss a female employee assisted with the plan. Most likely the male boss would ignore it and tell the male manager not to mention it again.

We have already discussed some points where I believe women would improve our workplace environment. This is the very essence of why I believe women should have more power. Men have proven for thousands of years that they are incapable and need a woman to even get out of bed in the morning. How many things could we accomplish in only a few years if men were able to take care of themselves and finally recognize the value women have in leading our businesses and our country?

Accomplishment

Can you accomplish everything discussed in this book? Absolutely! And with little or no effort on your part. After all, you are the king, ruler of all, top dog, master of your abode, *right*? Now that I have reminded you that you said you are the boss, then accomplishing a few small tasks on a daily basis shouldn't be too tough for a giant among men such as yourself, *true?*

Nothing I've talked about here is difficult. It is simple courtesy to another human being to whom you pledged your life forever, a person who gives the totality of her soul to you every waking moment.

She is a person I assume you profess to love. Why would you not want to give everything possible to this person? Giving is a personal thing, so remember the words *You receive what you give* are true.

Try it for a few weeks. Pay close attention to the behavior of the people around you. Their behavior will change, all because you took that first step and made that first respectful giving gesture.

If you are saying to yourself, *"Women should take that first step,"* you need to realize that they do every single day. You refuse to respond to them and you refuse to acknowledge them. Your spouse or girlfriend does countless tasks for you every day. Are you paying attention? *She is.*

Reason

Why should you do these things? To show the person you love that she is the most important person in your life. To show the world that you, the "big man on campus", are not afraid to let everyone know she is the most important person in your life.

Why *shouldn't* you do these things? After all, everything we have discussed here is only being cordial, a trait that would make anyone a better person. Think of it—acts of kindness bestowed upon another person. *How wonderful is that? As if we needed a reason!*

Reward

What? You are expecting to be rewarded for being a kind, loving, thoughtful, selfless human being? If you truly are all these things, you would never expect a reward.

If you asked, "Is there a reward?" the answer would be "Yes." A simple word: *feeling.* The feeling you get when you see her smile, look into her eyes, hold her hand, and see the emotion in her well up because of your actions and words. Don't forget loving actions and the words she likes to hear you say, such as *I LOVE YOU. Tell her! Tell her often! Time is fleeting!*

Finally

You may be asking yourself, *"Does the author of this book, do all these things?"*

Answer: *No, not all of them.* I work on it daily. I use these words to remind myself, and I endeavor to improve each passing day. However, I feel very comfortable saying, *"If you ask my wife, my daughter and my female co-workers how they are treated by me, I trust their answers would be, 'He is better than most.'"*

When was the last time you heard a stranger say to you as you opened the car door for your wife, *"How very nice"*? Yes, it was a woman who spoke those words to me, and I said, *"Thank you!"*

Changing Now for the Good

There is evidence that is seen where men are treating women with more respect. I believe it is still very slow indeed, but change is astir. On any given day, without trying, you can be a firsthand witness to a continued imbalance and disproportion of women's roles in the workplace and beyond. From a simple television news program, where the male newscaster asks the man more questions than the woman, to blatant acts by male office managers expecting women to clean up the office break room or take notes during a meeting.

Changing, yes, but I believe real change won't come until more women are in key decision-making roles.

Challenge

If you are a man and you do not believe any of what you read in this book, here is a simple challenge: Test the reactions for yourself. Start slowly, in case you may not be able to handle the truth.

1. Ask a woman how women should be treated at home and the workplace. Then ask a man the

same question. Young or old; it makes no difference. Create hypothetical situations and ask each the same questions. Write down the questions and answers. You don't want to miss any details. You will be amazed with the results. *Please note I did not suggest you ask a woman to do this for you. If you fail to accomplish this small exercise, you will certainly need advance training, which will require a woman's touch!*

2. This may open your eyes a little further. If you have a daughter, ask her these questions:

    a. Do you think Dad should help Mom with getting everyone ready for school and work in the mornings?

    b. Does Mom do all the housework?

    c. Do you think Moms should go to work and Dads stay home?

    d. Do you think Dads should go to work and Moms stay home?

    e. What do you think Moms do at work?

    f. What do you think Dads do at work?

If you already aspire to treat women with respect, you only help yourself by asking some questions. Some men will understand and work to change, while others will continue to be those nightmares that Moms and Dads fear will assail their daughters.

If you fall into the larger category of "you don't need to change" then you can only hope there will be a woman willing to lead you out of the darkness.

Not All Men Are Bad

I must make the statement *Not all men are bad* because it is true. There exist in our world men of their word, men with righteous intent, men who openly and truthfully address women with respect. To those men, this book is a friendly reminder that we can always do more to overcome the inequities we see and strive to be the change necessary to assist our most cherished of companions to flourish both in life and in the workplace.

Everything in this book may be wrapped up in the essence of three words: compassion, love, and communication.

Compassion is a deep awareness of the suffering of another, coupled with the wish to relieve it.

Love means a caring compassion, with no thoughts of receiving a reward.

Communication is the exchange of thoughts, messages, or information, by speech, signals, writing, or behavior, between two or more persons, and the one and only requirement is that two persons begin a conversation.

We are talking about men here; therefore, use this handy road map as a daily reference. I am reminding those good men to keep up the good work *(Mom would be proud)*. I am reminding those other men to get a clue and remember what their Mothers have taught them their entire lives: *How to treat women with love, respect and the dignity they so richly deserve.*

About the Author

Mikal Haney grew up in the panhandle of Texas oilfields. He briefly attended West Texas State University in Canyon, Texas. Yet those oilfields were calling his name, and he was soon back where the term "white collar" was largely unknown. In those times, 19-year-olds not in school soon received a letter inviting them to serve their country. This led to 9-year "career" in the United States Marine Corp because Dad was a marine and there would be nothing else for Mikal.

After recruit training in California and five years between San Diego and Honolulu working within the Information Technology environment extending the knowledge he began in college, Mikal decided teaching was his forte and Parris Island, South Carolina, USMC Drill Instructor School was the place to hone his skills. A few recruit platoons later, having achieved the status of Senior Drill Instructor, he was off to Okinawa, Japan, because one simply does not spend two years as a USMC Drill Instructor and casually return to a former life. You need a little time to realize not everyone you interact with is a recruit.

Moving on after the Marine Corps, Mikal tried being a shift supervisor in manufacturing, but the staff were not recruits. Also, it was disturbingly apparent these jobs required workers to be outside in the heat of summer and the dead of winter, just like the oilfield. So back to his best knowledge base and skill set that he was trained for in the Corps, he got work in Information Technology, which was warm in the winter and cool in the summer. And there he stayed.

How did Mikal arrive at writing a book? Through encouragement from loving caring people in his life to tell his story his way.

www.ingramcontent.com/pod-product-compliance
Lightning Source LLC
Chambersburg PA
CBHW061652040426
42446CB00010B/1701